"Paul McCord has written the most complete sales bible for aspiring sales superstars I've ever read! His 12 Keys will become your "Ten Commandments" to both a far more profitable career and fulfilling life!"

Dave Anderson, best-selling author,
How to Deal with Difficult Customers

"Think top sellers are born, not made? If so, you'll learn otherwise in this straight-shooting book by Paul McCord. He takes the mystique out of their stellar results and shows you exactly what top producers do differently than the Average Joe. Best of all, he shows you how you can replicate their achievements, capitalize on your personal strengths and take charge of your success."

Jill Konrath, best-selling author,
Selling to Big Companies

"In SuperStar Selling, Paul McCord lays out a step-by-step program, that if followed, will result in success. Finally, a sales "how-to" book that really does show exactly how to do it."

Paul Flood, President,
Paul Flood Marketing, Fairfield, Ohio

"SuperStar Selling: 12 Keys to Becoming a Sales SuperStar is a must read for any independent business owner or sales manager charged with equipping a sales staff to write more business. This book provides a clear, detailed path for any owner or manager to guide their team to massive success."

Tom Baker, President,
Advanced Automation, Inc., Dallas, Texas

"This is a must read handbook for anyone wanting to go to the top in sales. If you want to make a mark in sales, I strongly recommend you not only read the book, but implement what you learn."

Nkechi Ali-Balogun,
Principal Consultant, NECCI Consulting, Lagos, Nigeria

"Advice worth twice the price from the man who wrote the book on how to build a business through referrals. A must-have for anyone looking to start from scratch or get to the top in their sales business."

Robert Haynes,
20 year Financial Markets Senior Executive, Boston, MA

"This should be a required read of any job seeker seeking a career in sales or any sales pro consdering a change."

Rob Halvorsen,
President, Sales Careers Online, Houston, Texas

"If you're still dreaming of becoming a sales superstar, or simply need to *finally* make a decent living, then this book will meet you where you are today, and show you the steps. No vague fluff. No impractical methods. Just training of the highest order. Paul's a 'Dr Phil' for no-nonsense sales training."

Dr. Martin Russell,
WordofMouthMagic.com, Australia

"An excellent and insightful piece of work, well researched and simply presented. The Twelve Keys that unlock the magic of sales mastery!"

Alan Todd,
RE/MAX, Canada

"Paul McCord provides a step-by-step approach for separating yourself from the crowd of faceless salespeople scrambling to survive. If you are ready to be a Super Star sales professional, buy this book, study its truths, and apply its powerful lessons for achieving outstanding results."

Randy Pennington, Author
Results Rule! Build a Culture that Blows the Competition Away

"Troubleshooting your career is the first step to change. Finding real solutions is the second. This book shows you how to do both to finally get the results you want."

Ted Timmers,
European Director, EuroTeam Import/Export Ltd.

Paul McCord

SuperStar Selling

12 Keys to Becoming a Sales Superstar

New York

SuperStar Selling

12 Keys to Becoming a Sales Superstar

by Paul McCord

ISBN: 978-1-60037-399-2 (Paperback)

Published by:

www.morganjamespublishing.com

Morgan James Publishing, LLC

1225 Franklin Ave. Ste 325

Garden City, NY 11530-1693

Toll Free 800-485-4943

www.MorganJamesPublishing.com

**Cover and Interior Design
and layout by:**
Bonnie Bushman
bbushman@bresnan.net

Acknowledgements

I want to thank my wife, Debbie, for putting up with me during the process of writing this book and allowing me to disappear into my home office for long stretches at a time.

Sammie Justesen of Northern Lights Literary Services, my agent, worked diligently to get the book published. Her husband Dee also provided critical feedback on early drafts of the book.

Additional early readers who gave feedback and helped shape the book include Jeff Blackwell of Sales Practice, Jan Visser of EyesOnSales, and Robert Hynes of UBS. I owe a debt of gratitude to each.

Special thanks to Dr. Richard Tuerk, Professor of English at Texas A&M University, Commerce, and Dr. Miroslav John Hanak, former Professor of Literature and Languages, who taught philosophy, also at Texas A&M, Commerce. More than teaching me literature and philosophy, these men taught me logic and critical thinking skills. I may not practice the skills well, but I owe these men a great deal of thanks as primary influences on developing what little skill I may have.

Table of Contents

Introduction:
Can You Learn to be a SuperStar?

Spectacular achievements are always preceded
by unspectacular preparation.
— **Roger Staubach**

What does it take to go from being an average or slightly above average salesperson to a superstar? Is learning prospecting and selling techniques and strategies enough? If so, then how do you explain millions of salespeople who spent years reading and studying all the prospecting and sales process books they could find, attending seminars and workshops, and listening to endless sales training tapes and CD's but have not progressed beyond average?

Moving from the middle to the top of the pack requires far more than simply learning a few strategies and techniques. Becoming a sales superstar requires learning how to reprogram your brain— how to go from *thinking* and *acting* like an average salesperson, to *thinking and acting like a superstar*. Superstars don't think nor do act like the average salesperson. I'm not talking about having a big ego, being loud and boisterous, or acting like a prima-donna. A few superstars have these unfortunate qualities, but most don't. They do, however, have many other characteristics in common.

The superstars of selling have learned to overcome their self-doubts and their internal inertia when faced with setbacks. Notice the word "overcome." Superstars are no different from you or any other salesperson. They, like you, fear failure. They have—

or had—the same self-doubts about their ability to succeed, to make enormous incomes, to establish themselves as experts in their field. They, like you, have had to fight paralysis when encountering setbacks.

Nevertheless, they have learned to confront and defeat the issues, the personal demons, and the inevitable failure all salespeople face. They have learned how to eradicate their personal limiting beliefs. They have learned how to take whatever resources they started with and use them to their best advantage. They have learned how to develop a mindset that doesn't limit their performance, their income, their goals, or their objectives. Although they may have started with the same limitations, lack of resources, and lack of skills as any other salesperson, they have learned the Keys to becoming a superstar. Superstars have learned either through trial and error or by astute study the 12 Keys to becoming a sales star that you are about to encounter in this book.

Often salespeople learn the "how" of some aspect of sales. They read a book or attend a seminar and learn how to use a particular technique or strategy. Then, they fail to implement it. Learning a skill is useless unless you put the skill into practice. Knowledge, in and of itself, will change nothing in your life or your career. It may allow you to answer a trivia question. It may give you comfort. It may even allow you to feel superior. Still, it doesn't change a thing. Only when you turn knowledge into practice does it have the effect of changing your life and your future.

The difference between superstars and the middle of the pack salespeople is implementation. Their knowledge is experiential, not just intellectual. They have taken what they have learned and made it a part of their life. They simply DO what they KNOW. Unless you take what you learn from the coming pages and implement it in your career, you'll not progress far past where you are today.

Vision without action is a daydream.
Action without vision is a nightmare.
— **Japanese Proverb**

Consequently, this is an action book. Read it. Digest it. Implement it. You obviously want to go from where you currently are to the top of your profession or you wouldn't be reading this book. In order to do that, you must commit yourself to taking each of these Keys and implementing them in your business. It will take time. It will take effort. It will take hard work. You cannot expect to change yourself and your business overnight, but with work and diligence, you can become the sales superstar you envision yourself becoming.

The Keys contained within are the "unspectacular preparation" Stuabach mentioned. Nothing you will encounter here will be glamorous. Most of it will require a good deal of work—and not particularly pleasant work at that.

This book, more than anything else, is about discovering what you are doing well and where you need change. Change is the core of the book. It is about changing yourself, your sales business, and your career. If you're looking for a book with easy answers, this isn't the book for you. If you are looking for a book that will teach you the "secret" techniques and strategies to making the sale or becoming rich, again, this book isn't for you. If you're looking for an easy to read, easy to implement workbook that will magically change your career, once again, this isn't the book.

This book, frankly, isn't for everyone. If you are not seriously committed to becoming a star in your organization and industry, you will find the material in the book to be boring, too difficult, and far too demanding. If you are happy just being one of the crowd, you may as well stop reading now because you won't do the exercises, you won't do the required in-depth self-evaluation, and you won't do the necessary preparation to become a star. Reading the book, then, is just wasting your time.

However, if you're looking for a guide to change your business and your career permanently, read on. If you're serious about real, substantial, income-producing change, read on. If you are willing to invest the time and the effort in analyzing your sales business and yourself as you are today and then to use that knowledge to create a sales business that will reward your efforts for a lifetime with the income you envision, read on.

Yet, as you work your way through each Key and begin to think it too hard, too difficult, or too laboriously detailed, keep in mind that the work you have undertaken is the underpinning, the foundation for creating the career you desire for yourself. *The work you do today becomes your success of tomorrow.* The more effort you put into working through these Keys, the faster your business will grow and the more solid will be your career's foundation.

One further note about the change you are about to undertake. As you work through the various Keys, you will notice that the book doesn't have any answers for *you*. The answers must be your answers, not mine or anyone else's. No one can complete the work entailed in this book for you. Direction can and is given. If you want someone to hand you the answers to success, you'll be disappointed. On the other hand, if you want success and are willing to work for it, you have the questions you must answer in your hand.

Making Your Sales Job Easier

> *The talent of success is nothing more*
> *than doing what you can do well...*
> — **Henry Wadsworth Longfellow**

If you want to be a superstar in sales, the formula is surprisingly easy. Simply find out what you do well and then find the product, the company, and the sales process that allows you to spend the majority of your time doing those things.

So easy. Yet, so difficult.

That's the crux of this book; that's the change we are aiming for.

What do you do well and how can you create your own sales business around those few things? How can you find the product or service that fits your strengths? How can you find the target markets, the marketing methods, and the sales process that cater to your strengths? How can you develop the mindset that eliminates the thoughts and worries that block your ability to use your strengths to their fullest?

Answer those questions and you will have found your personal Key to becoming a sales superstar. The 12 Keys are nothing more than a disciplined process to ask questions and help you discover your own individual Key. No two people will have the same experience with this book, for no two people will have the same Key to success. You can learn from one another. You can emulate one another to some extent. Nevertheless, none of you can be an exact duplicate of another. You must each forge your own path. However, forged well, that path can lead to discovering a sales career where the sales seem to come easily and often, not because of some magic that you have discovered, but because you have finally managed to match what you do well to what you do.

Where to Start

Each of the Keys is necessary to become a superstar in sales. However, only you know where to start your journey to the top. Each Key stands by itself, yet they are all intertwined. Many of the Keys build on the discoveries you make in Keys 1 and 2. Consequently, it will be difficult to work through Keys 3-12 if you skip the first two Keys. Although you can accomplish one Key and ignore another, they are meant to work together as each is an integral part of your business' foundation. Whether you chose to complete each or not, you are making a choice. You are choosing to create a new foundation for the area addressed in that Key or you are choosing to accept what you are currently doing.

Eventually, you must read and fully implement each of the 12 Keys or choose to work from a weak foundation that may not withstand the trials and tests you will face in your sales business.

Take the book and turn it into your personal growth program. Working on your weakest area first may not be your best choice. Rather than focusing on your weakest area, focus on the areas that will produce the greatest return quickly.

Don't feel that you have to do all of your work at once. Read the book through once and then plan your self-change process over time. Work on one Key until you are thoroughly comfortable and then move to the next.

Knowing is not enough; we must apply.
— **Goethe**

Some Keys, such as coming to grips with your past sales history, require a great deal of detail work to reconstruct your sales and prospecting history. Others, such as the Key on client and prospect communication, require only that your future communications be addressed, so there isn't any "homework" to be done.

All of the Keys call for action. Whether that is reconstructing your sales history, analyzing and structuring your client and prospect communications, developing a superstar mindset and overcoming self-doubt, or deciding on your marketing strategies, each Key requires you to put into action what you learn.

Throughout the book, you'll find boxes with the target symbol 🎯. *Target boxes describe actions you need to take NOW.* Pay attention to the target boxes and perform the actions before moving on to another section.

One of the deadliest responses you can have once you read a Key is to blow it off because "I already do that." If you get to the end of the book and have that response to each of the 12 Keys and you aren't making an income in the top 20% of your industry, you had better rethink what you're doing. Because despite what you're telling yourself, you're not implementing the Keys.

You cannot learn and implement each of these 12 Keys and not become a top producer. It may take you months, even a year or two to learn and implement each Key. However, *if you diligently and fully apply these Keys to your career you cannot help but reach the top of your industry.* Why? Because you will be doing exactly what superstars do and if you do what the superstars do and do it well, you will become a superstar. The Keys to your success are in your hands. Now, it's up to you.

> *It's our choices that show what we truly are,*
> *far more than our abilities.*
> **— J.K. Rowling**

What You Should Have Learned

The last section of each Key summarizes what you should have learned about yourself and/or your sales business. "Summaries" do not summarize the Key, but rather the results of your personal actions taken during the process of working your way through the Key. Just as no one other than yourself can perform the action steps you must take, no one but yourself can determine whether you have applied the Key fully and correctly. However, the Summary will give you guidance to help you determine if you have been successful in the actions you have taken.

Examples

Throughout the book, you will find a number of real world examples of the principles discussed. There are both positive and negative examples. Because many of the examples are negative, I have chosen to use fictitious names for the salespeople and professionals involved. Rather than embarrass some and praise others, I think it best to let the example speak for itself.

For my clients and seminar attendees who recognize themselves in the examples, if you recognize yourself in one of the negative examples, your identity is safe. If you recognize yourself in a positive example, feel free to take credit with your family, friends, peers, and acquaintances.

Additional Resources

You will find additional tools and resources at http://www.thetwelvekeys.com, the companion website to the book. There you will find a continuously updated resource of articles, lists of training resources, including seminars, tele-seminars and workshops, along with other resource materials.

Don't Lose Sight of Where You're Going

As you get into the book, you may become overwhelmed with the work you're asked to perform. Some Keys such as Key 1, reconstructing your sales history, require a great deal of detail work that may seem either too difficult or even pointless. Yet, the work you perform in that Key is crucial for completing other Keys.

The few hours you spend on each Key will repay you many, many times over. Don't allow yourself to lose sight of your ultimate objective—transforming your sales business. Transformation and change is seldom easy. You are embarking on one of the most crucial transformation projects you will ever undertake. You can accomplish the task.

As you tackle each Key, know that you are working your way toward the career, the income, and the success you want for yourself and your family. The task is not the goal; it is your pathway to your goal. As you complete each task, you are closer to the success you seek.

12 Key Work Groups

Working through these 12 Keys is a major step for anyone. You may feel you need support and guidance as you go. You may need someone to help you work through particular areas and help you discover your Key.

I've found that working with others through these Keys cannot only give the support needed to stay on track, but can give much needed insight and direction.

If you would like a structured format for working through your plan, you can join a 12 Key Work Group. Each group is limited to a maximum of 20 participants. We meet one an hour a week for six months via the phone. Each participant is expected to maintain pace as the group works through the Keys. During the week, communication is via email. These 12 Key Groups are intense workgroups, so the pace is quick and the results quicker.

If you would like to participate in a 12 Key Work Group, you can register at <u>www.thetwelvekeys.com</u>/html/workgroups.html. Registration is $895 for the six-month session, less than $37 a week, less than a tank of gas a week, to change your career.

Key 1: Your Sales History: You Have to Know Where You've Been to Know How to Get to Where You Want to Go

If you want things to be different,
perhaps the answer is to become different yourself.
— **Norman Vincent Peale**

*B*ecoming a sales superstar starts with a thorough understanding of where you are right now in your sales business. The old joke, "you can't get there from here," isn't true, of course; however, what is true in sales, is this: You can't get where you want to go if you don't know where you are and *how* you got there. Unless you're willing to take an honest look at your prospecting, marketing, and sales activity, you will end up repeating the same mistakes you made in the past.

Performing an in-depth personal examination is never fun. Shining a light on what you've been doing as a salesperson may prove especially painful. Most salespeople have developed habits of lying to managers and peers—and even themselves—about their activities. If you are typical, your call report could well be renamed your non-call report. You, like many other salespeople, may pad your pipeline with fictitious prospects or "orders" to keep management off your back. Like many of your peers, you may rush through sales calls just to get them over with so you can chalk up another call on your report without giving yourself a legitimate opportunity to make a sale.

Unfortunately, you may have convinced yourself that you're as active as you proclaim yourself to be. If so, you won't be the first salesperson to participate in self-delusional behavior. You may be able to get away with lying to your manager and co-workers, but lying to yourself inevitably leads to failure.

Reconstructing your entire sales career is unrealistic unless you're new to your position. However, reconstructing a reasonable portion of your career, although difficult, is not only possible, but invaluable. By creating a history that honestly reflects your prospecting, marketing and sales activities, you can pinpoint areas where you have been successful; areas where you haven't met with a justifiable amount of success; areas where you failed; and areas where you simply didn't perform the required amount of activity to be successful. In addition, you will gather crucial numbers and ratios that will show you exactly what you must do to reach your goals and objectives.

Becoming a superstar means knowing what the superstars know—and they know their sales history inside out. Superstars know exactly what they do that works for them—and what doesn't. They know where they spend their time and energy. They know what each activity they perform is worth to their pipeline, their income, and their success.

Superstars know exactly what their time is worth. They know exactly what they must do to create the income they expect. They know exactly what they will be doing tomorrow, next week, next month. They know this because they know their history and every detail of that history.

If you want to be a superstar, you must follow their example.

Change is often uncomfortable, and self-initiated change only comes about when we recognize the need for it. Constructive change can only come after we recognize and define problems and opportunities. The act of recognizing and defining problems and opportunities in your sales business can only come from reliable data. Reliable data comes from your history. Superstars already have their data because they know they can't operate successfully without it. Now, you must catch up by generating your own data, based on your past activity.

For most salespeople, a year's activity will be a sufficient period to reveal tendencies, patterns, strengths and weaknesses. Newer salespeople who've been selling for less than a year have the advantage of having a less arduous task, but the results may not be as accurate. If you insist on shortcutting the work, don't examine less than the last six months activity. Even with six months you risk significant error due to the natural changes of the market, fluctuations in your personal selling activity, and other short-term factors that can skew the results.

Reconstructing your history involves investigating both your prospecting and marketing activity, as well as your actual sales numbers. You will be looking for:

- Where you spent your prospecting and marketing time
- The effectiveness of those activities
- Where your prospects have come from
- What resources you committed to each of your prospecting and marketing activities
- Patterns, if any, in the characteristics of your prospects geographic, income, gender, etc.

- Your closing ratio within each of your marketing channels
- Your average sales volume per sale and per month
- Your average commission per sale and per month
- The mix of products or services you're selling, if you sell more than one product or service

Information Gathering

Information is the heart of this Key. In order to understand how you arrived at where you are in your business, you must be willing to spend the necessary time to gather bits and pieces of information that will tell the tale. Unfortunately, if you're typical, you haven't kept a detailed record of your activities. Consequently, you will have to scrape to bring together the information you need.

A number of records are probably available to help you reconstruct both your marketing and sales history for the past year. The records and scraps of information you need to gather include:

- Pipeline reports
- Closed sale reports
- Call reports
- E-mails to prospects and clients
- Address books, both e-mail and telephone
- Notebooks, notepads and prospecting files
- Possibly your checkbook register
- Any other documentation that might help you identify prospects you dealt with and marketing activities you've engaged in over the past 12 months

Your objective is to bring together all sources of data that will help you identify:

- To whom you spoke
- How you found them
- Whether or not they purchased
- What they purchased
- The sales amount
- Your commission on the sale
- If they did not purchase, why

This is a big task. It's time consuming, unpleasant, and may be discouraging. But necessary.

During the following process of examining your past year or few months' history based on the information you manage to locate, you will need to be devastatingly honest with yourself. You may have padded your call reports in order to pacify your sales manager. If so, back out all the padding. You may have lied on call reports about what took place while meeting with a particular prospect (such as claiming the prospect could not afford the product or service when you know the real reason you didn't make a sale was because you blew the presentation). You will need to eliminate any false or inaccurate information.

> *Unless you change how you are,*
> *you will always have what you've got.*
> **— Jim Rohn**

Being honest in evaluating your activities is not pleasant, but without having an accurate picture of your history, it will be difficult—maybe even impossible—to identify and correct problems and recognize your strengths and opportunities. Keep in mind that no matter how uncomfortable you are with facing your true history, this is not an exercise in self-flagellation. Rather, it's the beginning of creating a superstar sales career.

Be creative as you search for your data.

Rita's phone bills: Rita, an independent representative selling insurance and financial products found herself with little data to go on when trying to reconstruct her year's history. She had reports from the companies she brokered for, along with some e-mail communications to prospects and clients, a notebook containing unorganized notes about various prospects, and files on her clients and a few prospects whose sales fell through. However, she had little to work on when it came to the marketing she'd performed during the course of the year.

Like many salespeople, she wasn't well organized. Once a prospect fell through, she tossed most of the communications away. Even worse, she didn't put prospects into her database until they moved from prospect to client.

However, she did have her check register and phone bills. Many of her better prospects she met for either lunch or coffee and she did make a habit of recording in her check register why she'd spent the money. Accordingly, her register helped her identify several prospects she only met once and then forgot about.

The most valuable data came from her phone records. She went month-by-month through her records, one phone number at a time. Most of the numbers were quickly eliminated, as they were the numbers of her family, friends, the companies she brokered for, and vendors she used for various products and services. She was left with several dozen numbers each month to investigate. Again, many were easy to identify, as they were numbers in her database of clients. Nevertheless, she still had a sizable list of unknown phone numbers for each month.

By using a reverse telephone directory, she quickly put a prospect's name with most of the phone numbers she couldn't identify. The rest she called and within a few seconds had identified the prospect.

Although the process took her several hours, Rita reconstructed most of year's contacts and prospects. Her dedication to the task was admirable and above average. This commitment and creativity allowed her to put a year's prospects on paper, even though she'd been lax about keeping records.

 Gather Your Data

Before proceeding to the analysis phase of this Key, you need to gather every piece of data you can find to help reconstruct your marketing and sales activities for the year. Your goal is to identify each and every prospect you spoke with, how you found them, and the disposition of the sale. Like Rita, creativity may be called for if you were not good at maintaining records.

Putting the Sales Numbers Together

Sales numbers are usually much easier to track than prospecting and marketing activities. Since you must do both, attack the easier of the two first.

Do you know your sales numbers? Not just your commission dollars, but all of your numbers?

Without these numbers you won't be able to determine a path that will help you grow. Again, you cannot get there from here if you don't know where you are—and how you got here. In this section you will analyze where you are. The next section will help you understand how you got here.

Our demonstration analysis will be basic. We need only stick to basic sales and marketing data and ratios. We will use only basic math and the conclusions we draw will be those that any reasonably intelligent salesperson could come to. If you don't have a marketing, statistics, or logic background, don't worry—you can do this.

Now that you've gathered your data, what are you going to do with it? You're looking to construct a year's worth of numbers (or the time you have chosen to research if less than a year). You will examine:

- Amount of your average sales

- Your average monthly sales volume

- Your average number of sales per month

- Your average commission per sale

- The specific products or services you sell

- The average number of prospects you see each month

- Your average close ratio

- Your average non-sold sales volume per month (what's left on the table)

Notice that we are ultimately looking for 12 month averages—your theoretical average month. In order to get to the monthly average, you will have to construct and then analyze your month-by-month history.

You will determine what columns to include, based upon your product/service and industry, but a basic spreadsheet with these columns should be sufficient for most people:

Month	Client/ Prospect	Sales Volume	Commission	Product/ Service	Declined

Fill in the spreadsheet with your data, working through each month. Include prospects who didn't purchase and customers. To differentiate clients from prospects, list clients in bold or use different colors for prospects and clients. Again, depending upon the industry, your spreadsheet may include several hundred entries or a few dozen.

Your finished spreadsheet will look like this:

Month	Client/ Prospect	Sales Volume	Commission	Product/ Service	Declined
Jan	Dave Song	$35,000.00	$490.00	mutual fund	didn't like
	Linda Henson	**$250,000.00**	**$1,200.00**	**whole life**	
	Carl Sauter	$80,000.00	$685.00	mutual fund	Competitor
	Barry Daniel	$500,000.00	$450.00	term	cost
	Dave Trips	$250,000.00	$185.00	term	Competitor
	Henry Wong	**$100,100.00**	**$820.00**	**mutual fund**	
Feb	Allison Harvey	$9,600.00	$960.00	health policy	cost

And so on throughout the year. Once your spreadsheet is finished, you need to drill down the results into month-by-month averages, adding a bit of additional information. Create a new spreadsheet that combines the results from your first spreadsheet:

Month	Products/ Services	Prospects/ Clients=Total	Volume Lost/Closed	Commission Lost/Earned= total	Reason Declined
Jan	mutual funds	2 / 1=3	115,000 / 100,100	1,175 / 820	1 didn't like 1 cost
	whole life	0 / 1=1	0 / 250,000	0 / 1,200	
	term life	2 / 0=2	750,000 / 0	635 / 0	1 cost 1 competition
Jan totals	3 mutual funds 1 whole life 2 term	4 / 2=6		1,810 / 2,020= 3830	1 didn't like 1 cost 2 competition

Thus, work your way through the year. In this spreadsheet, the first set of numbers in the prospect, volume and commission columns are prospects who did not buy. The second set, separated by the forward slash, are people who became clients and purchased. If you find it easier you can make two spreadsheets: one for clients and one for prospects who failed to purchase.

The spreadsheet is composed of only objective information with the exception of the last column. In many instances, the reason the prospect didn't purchase will be a guess on your part. You often know exactly why a prospect decided not to purchase, but if you don't know, make an educated guess. If you simply have no idea, record "don't know." You want your history to be as accurate as possible and just taking a wild guess won't help you spot issues.

Once you complete your monthly averages, you'll be ready to create your theoretical average month. Let's finish the above example by dropping down to the last row of the above spreadsheet, where the salesperson has added all of his monthly numbers:

Month	Products/ Services	Prospects/ Clients =Total	Volume Lost/ Closed	Commission Earned/lost= total	Reason Declined
2006 totals	57 mutual fund 4 whole life 21 term 12 health	48 / 36 = 84		72,198 /33,960 = 106,158	11 didn't like 14 cost 23 competition
Month ave	4.75 mutual fund .33 whole life 1.75 term 1 health	4 / 3 = 7		6,016.50/2,830 =8,846.50	.91 didn't like 1.16 cost 1.91 competition

Because of the nature of the products this salesperson sells, we didn't include an average monthly gross sales volume in the report. Since two products are based on dollar volume—dollars to invest and insurance policy face value, and one based on premium amount—health insurance, we ignored these numbers. If your product or service lines allow for direct comparisons, then these numbers should be averaged also.

Although this is a simplistic example, we can deduce a number of things about this salesperson:

- The close ratio is 42.8% (that is, he closed 42.8% of the prospects he met with — 36 sales divided by 84 gross prospects)
- The average commission per client is $943.33 ($33, 960 gross income divided by 36 sales)
- He met with an average of 7 prospects per month (84 prospects divided by 12 months)
- He closed an average of 3 sales per month (36 sales divided by 12 months)

- He lost an average of $6,016.50 a month in potential commissions ($72,198 lost income divided by 12 months)

- He tried to sell 68% of his prospects mutual funds; 4.7% whole life insurance; 25% term life insurance; and 14.2% health insurance

- Of the 48 lost sales, he lost 23 (47.9%) to competitors; 11 (22.9%) because the prospect didn't like the product they presented; and 14 (29.17%) because the prospect thought the product was too expensive

We could also examine the month-by-month results to look for patterns in the salesperson's performance. For instance, we might have found his above average months occurred all within a certain period, say, summer or fall. Or, possibly, he developed a pattern of bad month, bad month, good month indicating that once he had a pipeline of clients, he quit prospecting in order to service these clients. Once those sales were completed, the salesperson would begin prospecting again to load up his virtually empty pipeline.

What can we glean about this salesperson from the numbers? A great deal of important information:

- The closing ratio is not bad, at 42%. It isn't the greatest in the world, but it indicates he has a viable sales process that needs to be worked on, but is far from hopeless.

- He doesn't see nearly enough prospects a month in order to become a superstar.

- Either by accident or intent, he appears more comfortable selling mutual funds than insurance. When he does sell insurance, it's usually term insurance.

- He saw 84 prospects during the course of the year, but only presented 94 products, meaning he only presented more than one financial solution to 10 prospects at the most. That's only 12% of the prospects with whom he met.

- Almost 50% of his sales were lost to competitors, raising questions about

  ❖ his ability to establish relationships with prospects

  ❖ his ability to address the prospect's issues in a manner that makes sense to the prospect

  ❖ or the quality of the salesperson's products or service

- In combination with the above, almost 23% of sales were lost because the prospect didn't like the product(s) the salesperson presented. Again, this raises questions about either the salesperson's understanding of the prospect's issues and wants, or the salesperson's product line.

- The salesperson closed 36 sales with an average commission of $943.33, but failed to close 48 sales with an average commission of $1,504.12. He is losing the large, more profitable sales and closing smaller, less profitable ones. Again, this could be due to the quality or price of the product line, or it could point directly to the salesperson's comfort level in presenting products that require a larger investment or produce a larger commission.

This analysis raises a number of questions about this salesperson's business. But before we begin to draw conclusions about his activities and effectiveness, we need to look at his prospecting and marketing activity.

> **Develop Your Sales Numbers**
>
> Before analyzing your prospecting and marketing numbers, complete your sales numbers as above. If you wish, go one step further by examining the average monthly sales volume per product line, both closed sales and sales lost due to fallout. The more data you can gather and analyze, the more you will learn about your business so you can make appropriate adjustments.

Dennis' False Hope: Dennis, a coaching client of mine from the financial services industry, decided he didn't have the time, patience or need to reconstruct a whole year's history. Rather, he took a shortcut and reconstructed only a few months from the past year. He created his spreadsheets, analyzed his numbers, and emailed his results to me.

At our next coaching session before we got into his numbers, I questioned him about why he chose the five months he analyzed, since they weren't in chronological order. He told me he believed these were his most typical months. Rather than continuing the session, I instructed him to complete the exercise with all 12 months for the next week's discussion.

He completed the assignment and emailed it to me shortly before our scheduled meeting. The difference between his first analysis and his second were astounding. His first analysis included the five months he believed were typical of his performance, but they also happened to be his best five months of the year. The analysis of these months indicated he had a 53% close ratio; was seeing almost 22 prospects a month (about one per day) and earning an average of $8,400 per month. However, his full year spreadsheet showed his closing ratio was actually in the 28% range, he averaged seeing only 13 prospects per month, and his average income was just under $5,150 per month. A huge difference.

Had he continued using the numbers from his five-month analysis, any planning and projections he made based on that analysis would result in great disappointment, since his real closing ratio was about half of what his shortcut analysis indicated. In addition, he was seeing 40% fewer prospects than his original numbers showed—and his income was almost 40% less than in his original analysis. Although he knew his income was less than his original analysis indicated, he still believed his close ratio and the number of prospects he saw were fairly accurate, because those months were what he *believed* his typical month *should* have been. In other words, he chose to believe his best months represented him better than his actual averages did.

Nice thought, but it doesn't matter what he thought he could do. *What matters is what he actually did do.* Don't allow yourself to fool yourself. In a future Key, we will talk about beliefs, motivation and goals. But in recreating your history, you must deal with the reality of your history is, not what you think it should have been.

Putting the Prospecting and Marketing Numbers Together

If you don't want to do something, one excuse is as good as another.
— Yiddish Proverb

You probably find yourself spending most of your time looking for your next client. Most salespeople do. For most salespeople, selling is more about finding prospects than the actual sales process. Yet, salespeople seem to hate prospecting and marketing.

Finding prospects is the area where you'll try to fool yourself into believing you're investing more time and effort than you actually put forth. We salespeople are notorious for overestimating the amount of effort we invest in prospecting and marketing, while underestimating the amount of prospecting and marketing we must do to succeed.

The process of putting this data into a usable form is similar to that above. The primary difference is in the data you will put into your spreadsheet. As above, start a simple form with the following columns:

Month	Prospect/ Client	Marketing Channel	Marketing Method	Disposition

Obviously, you can simply copy and paste the month and prospect/client data into the table from your previous table. The three new columns are:

Marketing Channel: For our purposes, we will define a marketing channel as a distinct segment of people or companies you targeted during the year's marketing. (If you are on the marketing side of the business, forgive me for stealing one of your terms and redefining it). That is, distinct groups of prospects and clients such as consumers, referral partners, orphan clients of the company, or Internet shoppers. For example, if you are a mortgage loan officer, you might target four distinct groups:

- consumers looking to purchase or refinance a home
- realtors who could refer customers to you
- current and past clients who could refer you to new prospects
- Internet shoppers looking for a mortgage (a specific subset of consumers)

A loan officer would have many more potential marketing channels, but you get the idea. For each of the clients and prospects in your list, indicate the marketing channel where they belong. Even though during the year you didn't consciously direct your marketing efforts to specific channels or target groups, that's what you were doing. Identifying what channels brought you the most business, which were cost effective, and which weren't, is a necessary step to help you determine where your strengths and weaknesses lie, as well as indicting where you might want to consider spending more—or less—time and energy.

Marketing Methods: Marketing methods are the tools and strategies you used to reach the prospects and clients within each channel. Whereas marketing channels are the distinct groups you are trying to reach, marketing methods are how you get to them. Going back to the mortgage loan officer example, he may have used various methods within each channel:

- Marketing Channel: direct to consumer
  - ❖ Marketing Method: direct mail
  - ❖ Marketing Method: cold calling
  - ❖ Marketing Method: newspaper advertising
- Marketing Channel: realtors
  - ❖ Marketing Method: cold calling

- ❖ Marketing Method: visiting open houses

- ❖ Marketing Method: e-mail campaign

- Marketing Channel: client and prospect database

  - ❖ Marketing Method: e-mail campaign

  - ❖ Marketing Method: postcard campaign

  - ❖ Marketing Method: personal phone calls

- Marketing Channel: Internet shoppers

  - ❖ Marketing Method: e-mail campaign

  - ❖ Marketing Method: pay per click advertising

As you can see, you may end up using the same methods for a variety marketing channels. Particularly with marketing methods you used, the more detail you insert into your table, the better.

For example, if you received a prospect due to a response from your advertising, it's helpful to know it was an advertising response. However, let's assume during the course of the year you ran eight advertisements in three different publications. If you can narrow down the publication where the prospect saw your ad, you'll be able to generate better information for your analysis. Likewise, if the prospect came through a referral, knowing who referred them will help with marketing channel and methods decisions in later Keys.

Disposition: The disposition—that is, whether the prospect became a client, is also needed. Now your table now looks like this:

Month	Prospect/ Client	Marketing Channel	Marketing Method	Disposition
Jan	Dave Song	Orphan file	Direct mail	no sale
	Linda Henson	direct to consumer	direct mail	sale
	Carl Sauter	direct to consumer	cold call	no sale
	Barry Daniel	chamber of commerce	referral from Henderson	no sale
	Dave Trips	Don't remember		no sale
	Henry Wong	direct to consumer	direct mail	sale
Feb	Allison Harvey	chamber of commerce	networking	no sale

As with the sales table above, the salesperson will work his way through each of the 84 prospects he identified. Each prospect is classified by marketing channel and the method used to reach them, unless the salesperson cannot remember. Rather than taking a wild guess, if you can't identify with reasonable assurance where and how a prospect was brought into contact with you, simply mark it as "don't know." Usually your "don't knows" will be prospects with whom you had little contact. Possibly, as in the insurance salesperson's situation above, he quickly identified Dave Trips as uninsurable and consequently spoke with him for only a few minutes.

As with the sales spreadsheet, you will total your numbers in another table on a month-by-month basis, with a final summary of the results:

Month	Marketing Channel	Prospects/ Clients=Total	Marketing Method	Disposition Lost/ closed=Total	Close Ratio
Jan	direct to consumer	1 /2=3	direct mail	0 / 2= 2	100
			cold calling	1 / 0= 1	0
	orphan files	1 / 0=1	direct mail	1 / 0= 1	0

	chamber of commerce	2 / 0= 2	referral Henderson	1 / 0= 1	0
			networking	1 / 0= 1	0
Jan totals		4 / 2= 6		4 / 2= 6	33%

Then, the year's summary:

Month	Marketing Channel	Prospects/ Clients=Total	Marketing Method	Disposition Lost/ closed=Total	Close Ratio
2006 totals	direct to consumer		direct mail	14 / 9= 23	39.13%
			cold calling	8 / 3= 11	27.27%
			advertising	7 / 5= 12	41.66%
		29 / 17= 46			36.95%
	chamber of commerce		referral	5 / 9= 14	64.28%
			networking	4 / 1=5	20.00%
		9 / 10= 19			52.63%
	orphan files		direct mail	5 / 3= 8	37.50%
			e-mail	3 / 2= 5	40.00%
			cold calling	2 / 4= 6	66.66%
		10 / 9= 19			47.16%
	2006 Grand total	48 / 36=84			42.86%

As with the sales spreadsheet, we can distill a wealth of information from the prospecting/marketing spreadsheet:

- The most effective marketing channel in terms of closing ratio is the Chamber of Commerce, where he is losing just over 50% of the prospects he uncovers.

- The least effective in terms of closing ratio is direct to consumers.

- Direct to consumer produced almost 50% of the sales.

- Within the direct to consumer channel, direct mail and advertising perform at about the same rate, with cold calling lagging far behind.

- Although two expensive marketing methods—direct mail and advertising—have combined to generate 17 of the 36 sales for the year, the combined close ratio is only 39.53%. Cold calling, networking, generating referrals and email, which are inexpensive, combine to generate almost 53% of the sales, with a combined close ratio of 46.34%.

- It appears the two most profitable marketing channels, the chamber and orphan files, may be underutilized. In order to determine whether this is true, we would need to know how much time, effort, and financial resources were invested to generate prospects within each channel. These appear to be significant avenues for generating business.

The natural question is: Why would this salesperson continue to pump time, energy and money into a direct to consumer campaign while not stepping up the orphan file campaign? Salespeople have a tendency to aggressively pursue the channels they *feel* are generating the most business, even if that channel is less effective and efficient than another channel where they have invested few resources, but are generating higher average returns. Without an analysis of each channel, you cannot make rational decisions about your sales business. This salesperson apparently "felt" he was getting the most bang for his buck through the direct to consumer channel, because that's where most of his prospects (55%) came from. Yet, he may have been ignoring a far more efficient and less expensive channel simply because he had not invested enough resources in that channel to effectively mine it.

Tom's Folly: Sometimes you get into a rut and just don't have the will or desire to change. Tom, one of my seminar attendees, finished his personal history and discovered he'd been investing a tremendous amount of time and money in a direct mail campaign targeting small-to-midsize architectural design and engineering companies. Tom sells sophisticated reproduction equipment and these two industries are prime targets.

During his analysis, he discovered he had a much higher closing ratio when he spent his time and energy networking through various organizations, and even by cold calling. Yet, because of his marketing efforts, most of his prospects were generated through direct mail.

His analysis indicated that if he invested more resources in networking and cold calling he could increase his production by 30 to 40%, possibly more. However, the change would require him to invest more of himself, in the sense that both these prospecting methods required significant one-on-one involvement with prospects. On the other hand, his direct mail campaign brought in warm leads without having to engage them directly until they showed interest in his products.

Despite the evidence from the data, Tom chose to continue the direct mail campaign as his primary marketing channel because he didn't want to face the "no thanks" responses he received while networking and cold calling. He was more comfortable with an impersonal prospecting method where rejection was silent and he heard from lukewarm prospects he could convert into a sale.

Ultimately, Tom's analysis wasn't useless. He discovered areas where he could potentially increase his sales and income, but consciously chose to continue his old ways, knowing his results would probably be about the same as in the past. He knew his limitations and decided he was more comfortable staying in the familiar groove instead of stretching himself to grow his business in a new direction.

Of course, knowing is not enough. You must have the desire and commitment to change if you want to progress and become a sales superstar. Like Tom, you can consciously choose to remain where you are. On the other hand, you can make a commitment to become the superstar you can be. The choice is yours.

Develop Your Prospecting and Marketing Numbers

Like our mythical salesperson above, create your spreadsheets and carefully recreate your prospecting and marketing history for the past year. Take your time. Rushing through this exercise will not do you any good. If you are not willing to take the time to be thorough, there's no reason to go through the exercise. You need to create the most accurate picture of your activities you can put together. Only the most accurate picture will allow you to change your future. You cannot change the negative to positive unless you identify the problem. In addition, much of what you discover here will be the foundation for activities with future Keys.

Preparing for Next Year

This is not a one-time exercise. You will need to reevaluate yourself during the year and then complete a full historical review before preparing your next plan. Thankfully, your reevaluation and next complete review won't be nearly as difficult as your first.

By keeping accurate records during the course of the year, you can save yourself many hours of information gathering the next time you confront this exercise. A few minutes each day updating your information will ensure your records are accurate and easily available.

The information you need to record is basic and simple:

Date	Prospect/ Client	Marketing Channel	Marketing Method	Product/ Service	Commission	Disposition

When completed, this short form will contain all the information you need to analyze your numbers, including why each prospect declined to purchase. If you're diligent about keeping this marketing and sales information current, you should be able to construct your numbers and look for patterns in less than hour.

Summary

One faces the future with one's past.
— **Pearl S. Buck**

You have worked your way through your sales and marketing numbers. What now? What's the purpose of doing this?

As you will see in the Keys to come, the information and knowledge you gain about your history will impact your view of yourself and your potential, plus the changes you'll make to marketing and sales training. In addition, the numbers you've uncovered are the starting point for sales and income projections that will become part your personal marketing plan.

At this point, you should have a good idea where you and your sales business are and how you got there. You know your closing ratio with various marketing channels and methods. You know what channels you've been working. You know where you've been spending your time, money and energy. You know what worked, what kind-of worked, and what did not work.

Certainly there is much more to learn. The next Key will help you discover more strengths and weaknesses. Key 4 will help you explore new marketing channels. Key 5 will help you examine different marketing methods. In Key 6, you'll use the ratios you discovered in this Key to help you make solid sales and income projections. Key 9 will show you how and where to get the training you need to develop your skills, improve your strengths and overcome your weaknesses. Everything builds upon your work in this Key.

That doesn't mean you walk away from this Key with nothing but data.

Unless you change, you will stay exactly where you are. Our salesperson in the examples above now knows a good deal about his business. He knows he must look at his activity level if he wants to increase sales and income. He knows certain areas have a much higher close ratio than other areas. He knows what marketing methods are inexpensive, yet worked even better than more expensive methods. He knows he's closing his less profitable prospects, and he lost 23% of his prospects because they didn't believe his product met their needs. He presented more than one product to only 12% of the prospects, which probably limited sales and contributed to the fact that he failed to meet the prospects' needs and wants.

Like the salesperson above, you should now have a significant list of discoveries about yourself and your business. You should be able to identify potential strengths and weaknesses in your business.

Our friend above can draw several conclusions that will immediately increase his sales:

The most effective marketing methods he used involved personal interaction with the prospect. Both generating referrals and cold calling resulted in a closing ratio of over 60%, while the more impersonal methods of direct mail, email, and advertising hovered in the range of 40% close ratio. This salesperson evidently relates well to prospects on a one-to-one basis.

He concentrated on his least effective marketing channel.

Based on losing about 73% of prospects because of competition or because he didn't present a product the prospects felt met their needs, he needs to improve product knowledge, listening and comprehension skills, and presentation skills.

What discoveries have you made about yourself and your business? If you answer is "none," then you deserve congratulations, because you had obviously done this exercise before reading the Key. If your answer is "none" and you haven't performed this exercise before, either you didn't do the exercise well or you are lying to yourself. It's impossible to examine your sales history in detail without discovering new information. Some of your discoveries may reinforce what you suspected. If so, then you have the empirical data to back up your suspicions and can proceed knowing what you thought was accurate was, in fact, the case.

Many of your discoveries will be surprises. The response of "Huh, it sure didn't seem like that!" is common. For example, our insurance friend in the above example was probably surprised to find he missed the mark by continuing to pour time and money into direct-to-consumer marketing when other channels actually produced the most prospects. Without analyzing what was effective, he would never have discovered which profitable areas to concentrate on—*even though it didn't feel that way before the analysis.* He would have continued down the same path, with the same results.

Finally, the quote everyone has been waiting for in this section:

Those who cannot learn from history are doomed to repeat it.
— George Santayana

You now know what you want to continue doing and what must be changed. Your challenge is to find the will and the way to change those negatives.

Additional Resources

The sales and marketing history examined in this Key is of necessity short and simple. We don't have the space and most readers don't have the patience to work through a complete history and analysis. However, if you would like to see a full historical summary and analysis, you can find one at www.thetwelvekeys.com/html/history.html.

n, finding a mentor who understands metrics ze them, or working with your sales manager can ruct your history, discover patterns, and determine it to place more time and energy. You don't have to go . If you would like help in working through these Keys, consider a personal coach. In a later Key, coaching will be discussed in detail, but if you feel you need more guidance now, consider joining a 12 Key Work Group at <u>www.thetwelvekeys. com/html/workgroup.html</u>. If you would like personal one-on-one coaching, you can find my personal coaching philosophy at <u>www. thetwelvekeys.com/html/coaching.html</u>.

Key 2: Knowing Your Strengths and Weaknesses

We don't need more strength or ability or greater opportunity.
What we need is to use what we have.
— **Basil S. Walsh**

Do you know what you're good at? Do you recognize your strengths? Do you know where your weaknesses lie? Are you ready to change your sales business so you can take full advantage of your strong points and downplay your weaknesses?

Knowing your strengths and weaknesses not only helps increase your closing ratio and, thus, your sales; it can make your sales life easier and more enjoyable.

Obviously, not all superstars are alike. Some are outgoing; others are shy. Some are technically inclined, while others have little or no interest in details. Some seem to have a natural knack for effectively using the phone, while others are more effective in person. Some excel when selling one-on-one; others perform best in large, formal group presentations. Some are uncomfortable selling concepts and need a tangible product, while others prefer selling intangible products and services.

These preferences and personality traits contribute to each salesperson's success or failure. They will either enhance your natural abilities, or set up roadblocks to success, depending upon the products and services you're selling, the marketing channels you're selling into, the marketing methods you use, and the selling process you employ.

What strengths and weaknesses influence your ability to become a top performer? Fortunately, almost any man or woman can become a superstar—if he or she matches his or her strong points to the right product or service, marketing channel, method, and sales process.

add

Examples of the strengths you might identify include:

- Establishes strong relationships with prospects and clients
- Able to gather, digest and understand technical information quickly
- Ability to persuade
- Able to recognize, analyze and solve complex problems
- Sees the "big picture" and the relationship of things and people within that picture
- Develops a high level of trust quickly
- Able to work within a highly structured, formalized sales setting (call center type of setting where the structure is rigid)
- Can bring people of differing opinions and perspectives together
- High degree of self-discipline
- Ability to establish and meet goals
- Aggressive
- Persistent

Of course, you may have other strengths, in various combinations and to varying degrees. The person who works well in a highly structured environment may excel in a call center, yet struggle and fail in a situation with little formal structure, such as in an outside sales position.

On the other hand, a person with the distinct ability to recognize and solve intricate problems may thrive when selling complex products or services to corporations, yet be incapable of selling in an environment that lacks intellectual challenges.

Benton Smith and Tony Rutigliano in their book *Discover Your Sales Strengths* (Business Plus, 2003), claim the Gallup organization's research of over 250,000 sales people indicates that sales success is more intimately tied to connecting a salesperson's strengths to the right product and the right process than to any other factor, including experience and training.

Matching your strengths to what you sell, whom you sell to, and how you sell, can change your performance almost like magic. Likewise, finding the products or services, channels, methods and process that eliminate or at least mask your weaknesses can also have a dramatic and immediate impact on your sales.

Different products and services require varied strengths and can mask or allow for different weaknesses. Selling a complex networking solution takes different strengths than selling automobiles. Selling in a long sales cycle calls for different strengths than selling a one-time close product or service. Selling to a committee of decision makers in a formal boardroom setting takes different strengths than selling to an individual in his living room. Someone who can sell the devil out of carpet cleaning might be a complete failure at selling securities. Another who's a top performer selling financial services might be only average—or worse—when trying to sell or lease heavy machinery.

Understanding and aligning your weaknesses with your product and process can also increase your ability to succeed. We often make two mistakes in handling weak areas:

The first is to ignore them, as Smith and Rutigliano recommend in their book. They believe it's more profitable to concentrate on strengths and let our weaknesses take care of themselves. This ignores the fact that weaknesses can and do play a crucial part in our ability to succeed. Although your strengths may play the primary role in your ability to succeed, your weaknesses play an important secondary role—and if that role is large enough, it may cancel out your strengths.

The other common solution to dealing with weaknesses is to attack them head-on as the central issue in success or failure. What is the most typical outcome of a salesperson's annual review by her manager? She receives a list of weaknesses to correct or work on over the coming months. The manager may even set up a formal corrective program to help the salesperson address her weaknesses. Weakness and its eradication is the central focus of the review.

The key to any game is to use your strengths and hide your weaknesses.
— Paul Westphal

A more rational method is to identify weakness and find ways to mitigate it or turn it into an asset. For example, a salesperson that is impatient may be unsuited for a long sales cycle product or service, because he isn't prepared to work the process for months or even years before the gratification of a sale. Nevertheless, that same impatience may work in his favor in a one-time close environment.

Alternatively, a salesperson who's undisciplined and unorganized will probably have difficulty maintaining consistent, relevant follow-up with prospects and clients. In a sales situation where consistent, long-term follow-up is mandatory, this salesperson will soon face a crisis in her career. The standard managerial response is to encourage (or threaten) the salesperson, demanding that she work on and improve self-disciple and organizational skills. A more reasonable alternative is to mitigate the weaknesses by instituting an automated follow-up system where the salesperson's organizational skills and lack of discipline are minimized.

The idea that sales is sales and a superstar can sell anything is far from true. Yes, sales is sales, and everyone in this line of work has certain things in common, no matter what product or service they're selling. Everyone must find new prospects and contact those prospects, and then address a want, need, or problem the prospect has. And, we must close the sale. Yet, the mechanics and process of selling one particular product or service may be radically different from another, and call for unique strengths on the part of each salesperson.

Self-knowledge isn't easy to acquire. Many of us want to believe we have more positive traits, skills, and strengths than we actually possess. On the other hand, we also tend to exaggerate our weaknesses. That's why it's important to be realistic as we evaluate our abilities.

But how can we figure out our strong and weak points? Below you'll find a list of skills and behaviors to jump-start your thinking process. There are, of course, dozens more that you will need to consider:

- Patience
- Critical thinking
- Self-discipline
- Strategic thinking
- Problem solving
- Goal oriented
- Relationship building
- Oral communication
- Creative
- Persistent
- Consensus builder
- Persuasive
- Group presentations
- Inquisitive
- Team player

Some of the traits listed above are behaviors, while others are skills. Many of these characteristics may be a strong point in one situation and a weakness in another.

Results from Key 1

Obviously, one way to discover your strengths and weaknesses is to review the results of your activities in Key 1. Do you find a trait or behavior imbedded in the marketing methods that produced similar results? For example, the salesperson in our example discovered he did well when meeting prospects through referrals and networking. This indicates an ability to develop trust.

Furthermore, he also did fairly well with cold calling, indicating an ability to quickly connect with people.

Your marketing and sales history can reveal many strengths—and weaknesses. Do you find patterns that indicate you readily develop long-term relationships with clients—or do you perform better with a one-time close situation where you probably won't interact with the prospect again? Do your strengths appear to be intellectual, such as solving complex problems, or do you respond better to addressing the same issues in the same manner, with the same presentation, time after time? Does your history indicate you work well in a spontaneous environment (networking, for example), or in a more scripted environment such as cold calling?

Examining your sales and marketing history is an excellent starting point, but it's far from conclusive. You'll need to find additional ways to dig deeper.

Examine Your Sales and Prospecting Results from Key 1

Look for patterns in your sales history for strengths and weaknesses. List each strength and weakness with the intent of examining them further, using the methods below. Although your patterns are indicators, don't allow yourself to develop conclusions before you dig deeper.

Skill and Personality Assessments

A wide array of personality and skill assessment tools are available that can provide information about individual strengths, weaknesses, likes, and dislikes. Assessments try to help companies and individuals identify their personality and behavioral strengths and weaknesses.

Assessments should not be taken as absolute, although some companies use them that way. It isn't unusual for a salesperson to perform well on an assessment and then fail on the job. Likewise, others do poorly on the assessment and then excel when hired. Assessments are indicators, not crystal balls.

Taking a quality assessment tool can give you more insight into your personal strengths and weaknesses. Your sales history is your strongest indicator of your strengths and weaknesses but it cannot help you identify them all. In addition, it can be difficult drawing accurate conclusions from your sales history alone. You need additional input and an assessment is a great supplemental tool.

You needn't wait for a company to ask you to take an assessment. Assessments are available on the Internet at reasonable prices and they make useful coaching guides—either for your personal coach, your sales manager, or as a self-coaching mechanism.

One of the better sales assessments, although by no means the only good product, is the ProfilesXT Sales assessment by Profiles International. This assessment looks at your thinking style, behavioral characteristics, and occupational interests. It can help identify your strengths, thus helping you identify your "ideal" sales position.

Again, despite the assessment companies' claims, an assessment tool should be part of the big picture, not the final word. Assessment companies tend to market their products as gospel—or darn close to it. I've yet to have a religious experience with an assessment, but they should be an important part of your self-knowledge toolbox.

Most assessment tools, including the ProfilesXT Sales, have built in "traps" to help determine if you're trying to scam the test by giving answers you believe are correct. If you spend the money to take the assessment to improve your career, take the instrument honestly. If you try to dupe it, you're only cheating yourself. As with any computer program, an assessment depends upon the data we give it. Garbage in, garbage out.

Since the ProfilesXT Sales is one of the best on the market, I've made special arrangements with Gately Consulting for readers of this book to purchase the assessment at a discount and take it on-line, with virtually immediate feedback. Gately Consulting is a Boston based human resources consulting firm headed by Bob Gately. To request a PXT Sales assessment, send Bob an email at gately@csi.com with "McCord's PXT Sales Assessment" as the subject. Bob has graciously agreed to assist with any interpretation issues you may have, via e-mail at gately@compuserve.com.

Take the Profiles International ProfilesXT Sales Assessment

Take the ProfilesXT Sales assessment (or an equally good assessment of your choosing). Compare the results with the information about strengths and weaknesses you mined from the data in Key 1. If the assessment reinforces your discoveries in Key 1, you've probably found real strengths or weaknesses. If you found discrepancies, keep digging.

Manager Feedback

A less reliable, but potentially valuable resource, is your sales manager—especially if he or she is actively involved in your sales activity by going on ride along calls, reviewing your activity reports, and working with you on presentations.

Keep in mind you must weigh your manager's opinions based on a number of factors. Not all sales managers are capable of helping you take a serious look at yourself. Some may not have the experience; others may try to soft-pedal your shortcomings. In the worst case scenario, a manager may sabotage your research by giving a false analysis due to jealousy or disliking you. Use what you know about your manager and your relationship to determine the value of any input from that source. If you're fortunate enough to have a good, involved manager, her observations can be a great help.

Compare your manager's analysis to your assessment findings, and then to the patterns you discovered by analyzing your sales and prospecting history.

By starting with your personal history and then using formal assessment tools, manger feedback, and the other methods below, you're moving from the most concrete and reliable data to the least reliable.

Your Personal Likes and Dislikes

An even less reliable, but, again, useful analysis is looking at what you like to do—and what you don't like. Assessments try to address this issue also, based on the assumption that you will be good at—or at least become good at—the things you enjoy doing. Likewise, you are probably less accomplished at things you don't enjoy.

I believe there is a modicum of truth in this concept—but only a modicum.

I enjoy playing golf. I'm terrible at the game, but I love it. The truth is, I'll never be good at golf, because I don't have the talent—the strengths—necessary to become an accomplished player. If my performance matched my enjoyment level, I would be Tiger Woods. I'm not.

On the other hand, I've developed a simple system and enough personal discipline to guarantee I win at Craps most of the time. Virtually every time I play, I win more than enough to make up for what my wife loses playing Blackjack. Nevertheless, I hate playing Craps. I'm bored silly within 15 minutes, ready to leave the casino and actually do something. Debbie isn't. She loves to play Blackjack. Therefore, being the dutiful husband, I stay. I watch the poker players for a while. Then I watch Debbie play. Then I go back to the Craps table and play for a few minutes. Boring. Nevertheless, I am good at it.

Of course, I'm not arguing that you won't or can't be good at what you enjoy, I'm simply pointing out that there isn't an absolute correlation between loving doing something and being capable of being good at it.

Still, there's something to be said about engaging in selling a product or service or using a sales process that allows you to engage in activities you enjoy. Just don't confuse enjoyment with strength.

However, if you find your strengths align with your preferred activities, you have a strong basis from which to launch an aggressive and enjoyable new process.

Meet With Your Manager and Take Inventory of the Activities You Enjoy

Have a serious discussion with your sales manager, asking for an honest assessment of your personal sales strengths.

Then sit down with pen and paper and think about what activities you now engage in that you find enjoyable—and distasteful. Consider what activities you are not currently doing that interest you.

Another Assessment—Sort of

In their book, *Discover Your Sales Strengths*, Smith and Rutigliano refer salespeople to the Gallup organization's StrengthFinder Center, which offers a 180 question assessment to help identify their top five strengths (the StrengthFinder calls strengths "themes").

The assessment analyzes different sales strengths and provides a report highlighting your top 5 strengths out of 34 potential strengths the assessment is designed to identify.

The StrengthFinder uses unique terminology for the themes (strengths) it identifies. Terms such as Includer, Belief, Achiever, Focus, Learner, Responsibility and others are among the 34 identifiable strengths. Each strength has a short description. For example, the Harmony Theme is defined as, "People strong in the Harmony theme look for consensus. They don't like conflict; rather, they seek areas of agreement." Then, the Significance theme: "People strong in the Significance theme want to be important in the eyes of others. They are independent and want to be recognized."

Although the terminology used may be different, if you take the assessment you should be able to translate your dominate "themes" to match the strengths you've discovered—or to find a new strength you haven't uncovered.

Unfortunately, in order to qualify for the assessment you must first purchase the book, where you'll find a special code allowing you to take the test without further charge. Also, be aware that the assessment is part of Gallup's marketing campaign to sell additional training services.

Defining Your Strengths and Weaknesses

You should now have a great deal of information from a number of sources. What do you do with it?

Creating a "portrait" of your strengths and weaknesses should give you ideas about how you best relate to people, how you handle situations, and what activities you will perform best.

On a sheet of paper make two columns, one headed "Strengths," the other "Weaknesses." List each of the strengths and weaknesses you've discovered. At this point, don't worry about terminology. A little later, you'll combine like strengths and weaknesses into a single strength or weakness. Simply list each characteristic you've discovered, along with its source.

Your list might look something like this:

Strength	Weakness
Build relationships quickly (history)	obstinate (manager)
Learns quickly (manager)	lack of focus (manager)
Goal oriented (assessment)	hardheaded (wife)
Persistent (manager)	undisciplined (manager)

Work well with people one-on-one (history)	can be argumentative (manager)
Strong analytical skills (assessment)	opinionated (assessment)
Belief (assessment)	unyielding (assessment)
Problem solver (assessment)	
Logical Thinker (assessment)	
Independent (assessment)	
Understands complex issues (manager)	
Sell intangible services well (history)	
Connects quickly with people (history)	

Notice many of the weaknesses listed above can be strengths when expressed in different terminology. For instance, the strength of "belief," that is, having a solid base of core beliefs that you will not compromise, may also be described as "opinionated," a weakness. Likewise, the strength of "persistent" could be described in negative terms as "hardheaded" or "obstinate." As you can see, your strengths may also be your weaknesses, depending upon the circumstances.

The salesperson above can combine duplicated strengths and weaknesses. For example, he might place hardheaded and obstinate into a single weakness. Combining "logical thinker" and "sells conceptual services well" may be appropriate, even though they aren't identical, because selling conceptual services is often an intellectually challenging task, requiring the ability to think logically. In addition, it might be possible to include "strong analytical skills" with "logical thinker" and "sells conceptual services well," since analysis is also a task that requires the ability to think logically.

Perhaps you noticed inconsistencies in the above chart. The assessment describes the salesperson as "goal oriented," while the manager indicates the salesperson lacks focus. Does this indicate an error on the part of the assessment instrument or the manager—or is it possible for the salesperson to be both goal oriented and, at the same time lack focus? In this case, the salesperson needs to get a more detailed explanation from his manager to determine exactly what is meant by lack of focus.

After examining the results of his research, the salesperson created the following list:

Strength	Weakness
Quickly develops relationships with strangers	Lacks organizational skills
Recognizes, analyzes and solves complex problems	Tends to be uncompromising
Works best independently with well-defined goals	
Persistent	
Quickly masters complex technical information	
Thinks in concepts	
Has a strong moral compass	

Notice that when he created this final list of strengths and weaknesses, the salesperson boiled many strengths into a single statement—he can recognize, analyze, and solve complex problems, he quickly develops relationships with strangers, he quickly learns complex technical information, and he tends to be uncompromising.

This salesperson now recognizes seven strengths and two weaknesses that can be critical to his sales business. The next step is to analyze his current sales job and his sales process to determine:

1. if the products and services he sells are appropriate for his strengths and weaknesses

2. if he should he alter his sales process to take better advantage of his strengths

3. if he should change his sales process to mask or overcome his weaknesses

 Examine and Condense Your Strengths and Weaknesses

Analyze your original list of strengths and weaknesses and try to combine duplicates or similar traits into a single, comprehensive statement.

Matching Strengths to Product/Service: In the example above, the salesperson is oriented toward learning complex material, then using that knowledge to identify, analyze, and solve problems. In addition, he develops relationships quickly, prefers to work independently, and has a strong belief system.

What type of product or service would be an ideal match? Let's examine the strengths:

He likes an intellectual challenge—he handles this well and enjoys it. Most importantly, he's good at it. Based on the sales history, he seems to work best with conceptual sales as opposed to a tangible product.

Products and services that meet these criteria would include a consulting service, business-to-business software sales, sports, entertainment or literary agent, financial services sales, network sales, pharmaceutical sales, engineering or architectural sales, and financial products wholesale, among others.

Some of these professions can be eliminated because they require specialized knowledge or degrees, such as engineering, architectural, and network sales.

The salesperson above also works best in the role of a single hunter/killer, as opposed to working within a sales team. That would eliminate certain sales positions within the consulting, software and agent representative industries.

However, that leaves us with the financial services sector, many software positions, pharmaceutical sales, possibly some consulting sales, and agent representative positions as viable options.

Another major strength is the ability to identify and solve complex problems. Selling a fixed product such as pharmaceuticals, therefore, may not be a good match.

This salesperson also has a strong belief system that dictates he maintain a strong ethical base. Consequently, finding a product or service in which he believes will be necessary for his success.

He might be an ideal candidate for a long sales cycle product or service, or one with a long-term commitment.

Based on the above criteria, many financial services sales positions (financial planner, financial advisor, mutual fund wholesale) will fit. If the salesperson can find a software company that doesn't require a background in software sales, many software positions would work. A position as an independent entertainment, sports or literary agent would be a fit, but the issue of industry contacts could be prohibitive. In addition, selling consulting services would be a good fit, as long as the salesperson could work independently of the consulting team.

Based on the short-list of potential products/services, we have narrowed the field down to consulting, software sales, and the financial services industry. Had we taken more time to develop a potential list of products/services, we would probably end up with several dozen potential products/services that match this salesperson's strengths. Even with our short-list, this salesperson has many avenues to pursue, assuming his current position doesn't fit the above criteria.

Dan's New Found Success: In fact, the above scenario is the actual case of a salesperson who was misplaced in his job.

Dan held three sales positions before he worked on discovering his strengths and weaknesses. In each position he sold tangible products—autos, construction materials, and homes. He was miserable in each and barely eked out a living. He finally convinced himself he simply wasn't cut out to be a salesperson.

Yet, he excelled in one aspect of his real estate sales job, where his company sold add-on products such as home protection, warranties, and a couple of other items.

Even though his sales weren't that strong, the percentage of homebuyers who bought the extra services was far above the norm. He sold these additional small commission items well, much better than he sold homes. In fact, a few of his co-realtors asked him to help them present these add-on items to their clients. Despite the fact that these were small dollar items, his history indicated he was much more successful selling these than in selling homes.

He faced a number of issues with each of his previous positions. He was bored with the products and the sales process. With some, he was uncomfortable with the way the company demanded he sell. None gave him a sense of satisfaction or accomplishment.

After completing a rigorous examination of his strengths and his weaknesses, Dan elected to explore sales positions that matched his strengths. This process took a few months, but he eventually left his job selling homes and started as an inside salesperson selling client management software solutions to small companies. Within a year, Dan moved to an outside sales position where he is on track to become one of the top salespeople in his region.

Dan hasn't yet reached his ultimate income goal, but he's bringing in more money than ever before. He hasn't fully conquered his lack of organization, but the company he works for has a number of solutions that help keep him on track. Moreover, he is still learning his craft from a technical standpoint.

Yet, he is happy. He's making money. His sales are strong and projected to put him in the top 30% of the company by the end of the year. He fully believes in both his product and the solutions he develops for clients. No longer bored with sales, Dan believes he has found his niche.

Matching Your Strengths to Your Company: Not all companies are the same. Not all have the same structure or the same internal guidelines.

Finding your ideal product or service is only the beginning. If you are now selling a product or service that matches your strengths, great. If not, you need to make a move. However, beyond simply finding your ideal product or service, you must also find a company that will allow you to take full advantage of your strengths.

If you're an independent person who needs a great deal of freedom, but you're working for a highly structured company that allows for virtually no freedom, you will need to make a move. Conversely, if you need structure and work for a company with little or no structure, moving is on your menu.

Your choice of company is as important as the choice of product and service. Everything must match if you want to become a superstar in sales. If you have the perfect product but company restrictions keep you from exercising your strengths when marketing and selling, you'll fail just a surely as if you're selling a product or service that's totally mismatched to your talents.

If you need structure, find it. If you need freedom and independence, find it. If you need a team to work with, find it. If you need a company you can believe in wholeheartedly, find it.

Your strengths, and how you use them will take you where you want to go—not the product you sell, the service you sell, or the company for which you work. If you try to exercise your strengths is the wrong environment, you'll be mediocre at best.

> ### Find Your Ideal Products/Services/Company
> Condense what you have discovered about your strengths down to a few core strengths you can write as positive statements. Now, research what products and/or services match your core strengths. If these don't match your current sales position, think about a career move. If your current employer doesn't allow you to use all your core talents, find one that will.

Addressing Weakness:

Do not let what you cannot do interfere with what you can do.
— John Wooden

In addition to finding products/services that fit within your strengths, you must also address your weaknesses—finding ways to mitigate them, turn them into strengths, or address them head-on.

Ignoring weaknesses, as some advise, is dangerous. Concentrating all of your energies on them is equally dangerous.

One method for of addressing a weakness is learning how to diminish its impact. Dan, above, knows he's disorganized and has issues with making follow-up customer contact. He decided to find technology to help him address these issues without relying totally on his own devices. Fortunately, he joined a company whose product dealt with this very issue. Although his problem isn't completely solved, the technology carries about 70% of the load for him, giving him a head start on customer service.

Another alternative is to find a product/service or sales process that turns your weakness into a strength. For example, if you find you don't develop strong, lasting relationships or become bored when dealing with the same customers, yet you work well with people over a short period, moving from a multiple-contact sales cycle to a one-time close product or service will turn this weakness into a strength. Not only will you be happier, you will probably be a much better salesperson.

If you can't find a way to diminish the weakness or turn it into a strong point, you'll have to address it head-on and work diligently to correct it. In fact, even if you do find a way to mitigate your weakness, you still need to ensure it doesn't creep back into your life and harm your sales efforts.

For example, Dan found a partial solution to his disorganization, but he must follow through by actually using the new technology. That means entering data into the software and then giving it occasional instructions. In addition, he can't expect the software to do everything for him—the organizational tasks outside its capabilities are still Dan's responsibility. He addressed this issue by hiring me as a coach to help him focus on prospecting and marketing *and* overseeing his contacts and communications. I won't let him leave the office until he finishes the scheduling and contact activities for the day. In addition, we've added more automated resources to his sales toolbox.

How Will You Address Your Weaknesses?

Now you know what they are, although you probably suspected all along. How can you diminish, convert them to strengths, or change them? You must do one of the three—or some combination. Develop an action plan to address them right now and begin working on it while you're laying the foundation for your career success.

Selling Is not For Everyone:

What if you examined your strengths and don't see enough of them to help you excel in sales? Don't despair. Selling isn't for everyone. Many people in sales should be in another line of work. They hate everything about sales and selling. Their strengths and talents simply don't fit a career in sales.

To become a success in selling you need to align your strengths to your product or service, to the marketing channels you use, to the marketing methods you use, and your chosen sales process. You also need confidence and the correct mental attitude. Then, you must combine these attributes with commitment and desire to succeed. Strengths and talent are not enough. Neither are all the commitment, desire, and dedication in the world. Superstars have discovered how to combine their strengths and talents with a strong desire to succeed, a commitment to pay the price, and a firm belief that they will succeed. Not everyone can bring all of these factors into alignment.

If this is you, you certainly haven't wasted your time with the above exercises. Take what you discovered about yourself and perform the same analysis with the view of finding your ideal career—one where you will be happier, more successful, and better able to contribute to your family and company.

Summary:

By now you should have a solid grasp of what you do well and where your issues lie. You should know:

- Your core strengths
- Weaknesses that interfere with your ability to sell
- Which products and/or services match your core strengths
- Have a game plan to attack, diminish, or turn your weaknesses

Perhaps you discovered your strengths are perfectly suited to your current products or services. This makes life much easier. Now, your job is to find ways to make those strengths work for you. In later Keys, you'll discover how to find marketing channels and methods that will take full advantage of your strengths. You'll find ways to align your thinking and actions to your core strengths. You'll uncover ways to stretch yourself beyond your comfort zone and capitalize on what you do best.

If you discover you're selling the wrong product or service or you're with a company that limits your ability to utilize your strengths, it's time to take action. Take action today to begin the transition from where you are to where you can stand out. Lethargy is a killer. It will kill your career. It will kill your spirit. It will kill your soul.

Don't let fear or laziness keep you from taking action to get what you want from life. In a later Key, we will address this issue.

If you're afraid of making a move, immediately go to Key 12, "The Sales SuperStar Mindset," where you'll learn how to deal with your limiting beliefs and overcome fear and inertia.

Key 3: Committing to Your Career: What are You Willing to Invest?

The biggest mistake you can make is to believe that you are working for somebody else. Remember: Jobs are owned by the company; you own your career!
— **Earl Nightingale**

$\mathcal{M}$ost salespeople work on an undisciplined schedule. If they aren't required to show up in the office at a particular time, they arrive when they think they need to. If they don't have to stay until a particular time, they leave when they're finished. They may work 37 hours one week, 49 the next, 63 the following week, and then 32 the week after.

Salespeople tend to be undisciplined in other ways as well. They spend money on training one month, and then nothing for the next three months. They invest $75 in marketing one month, $30 the next, nothing the month after, and then $110 the month after that. In other words, their time, training, and marketing—their sales business—is run in a haphazard manner, doing what they *feel* needs to be done or spending what they *feel* needs to be spent.

This haphazard method of running a business is the exact opposite of what most superstars do. Superstars don't reach the top of their professions by accident. They're at the top because they developed a workable, effective plan of attack and then followed that plan, deviating only when new opportunities arose or when a portion of their plan stopped working.

Of course, life is more than a job and a career. We each have family, friends, and outside interests. We need time to recuperate and re-energize ourselves. And most of us work with a limited budget—often with commitments bigger than our wallets. Keeping all this in mind, if you want to become a sales superstar, you must decide exactly what you are willing to invest and sacrifice for your career in terms of time and money.

If you have the freedom to come and go on your own schedule, you're responsible for marketing and prospecting, and your company doesn't provide a boatload of top quality training, then you're far more likely to fail than a salesperson who receives more company support. That isn't an opinion; it's a fact. However, a position like yours can offer the greatest rewards to those who succeed. Most sales positions give you a tremendous amount of freedom. That freedom can be a great benefit, but for many it's a curse.

Few sales managers have the time or inclination to baby-sit salespeople, so they leave the decisions about when to come and go to the individual rep. A manager cannot force you to spend money on marketing, although he or she can certainly offer encouragement and help you determine where to spend your time and resources. Managers try to give as much sales training as they can, but most are poor trainers. Although they earnestly try to help, just like you, they're working with limited time, resources, knowledge, and skill.

In an ideal world, the company would support you with gobs of lead generation marketing. They'd overwhelm you with world-class training in all aspects of the sales process, from prospecting to customer service. They would provide support so you could concentrate on selling and bringing in new business. They would give you the resources you need so you don't have to spend a ton of money on marketing.

Few, if any, of us live in that ideal world.

The fact is, you must do far more than simply sell a product or service. You must find your own leads—or starve. If you want quality training, you must find and pay for it yourself. If you want to succeed in your sales position, you are responsible for your success, not the company. The company gives you the opportunity; it's your choice what to do with it. They supply the product or service; you supply the knowledge, time, energy, and most of the tools.

Despite what your W2 says, *you are not an employee. You are a mini company,* working exclusively for one client. If you want to succeed, you need to understand your position and take full responsibility for your own success or failure.

Disciplining Your Time

In selling, time is not your friend. Every salesperson, no matter how successful, lives from month to month; at the beginning of each month, the production numbers roll back to zero. On the first of each month, every salesperson in the world starts from exactly the same position—with no commissions earned, no sales made, and no honors, accolades or awards. If you want to keep eating, you have to do it all over again, month after month. Time, and how you use it, is ultimately your biggest challenge.

Managing time means managing your schedule, and as a company, you must have a schedule etched in stone. What quality company do you know that opens and closes on a whim? Can you think of any reputable companies that decide to close shop because they want to go buy a new pair of shoes? Or because they feel like playing golf? Or because the employees don't feel like working?

Nevertheless, you argue, those companies have dozens or hundreds or thousands of employees, so if someone is gone, others will keep the doors open. True. That, however, isn't the point. The point is, you have chosen to become a company, just like them. You have chosen to open your doors, and like any other company, you now have an obligation to be ready to serve your customers and clients within a structure they can count on.

However, just like any other company, you can establish your own structure. Store A chooses to be open from 9 to 9, Monday through Saturday; while store B establishes a schedule of 10 to 7, seven days a week. Each has the freedom to establish their own hours, but once they do, they must adhere to that schedule.

You have the same freedom—and responsibility.

What are you willing to commit on the road to becoming a superstar? Are you willing to work eight hours a day, five days a week? Maybe, eight hours a day, six days a week? Possibly ten hours a day, Monday through Friday and six hours on Saturday? How about ten hours a day, seven days a week?

Before you answer, think what'll be committing. How will you balance your career with your family? Your outside interests? With your friends? What tasks must you complete in your work?

- Are you responsible for marketing and prospecting? How much time will you need?

- Must you have to travel to your prospects and clients? If so, how much time will you lose to travel?

- How much time must you set aside for prospect and client meetings, including follow-up meetings?

- Once you make a sale, how much time must you spend on each client's purchase?

- For what non-productive tasks are you responsible? How much time do they take?

- How much time must you spend on prospect and client follow-up communication?

- Do you have to attend sales meetings? How much time do they take?

- How much time will you set aside for personal training?

- Does the company often require you to attend unexpected conference calls or meetings? How much time must you allot for these?

Few of us can accomplish all of these tasks in a straight 40-hour week. Yet, not many salespeople work 40 hours per week. How much time do you waste shooting the breeze with the other salespeople in your office? How much time do you spend doing busy work, such as designing the perfect flier, writing the perfect follow-up email, or checking on a customer's shipment instead of having someone in shipping handle it? How much time do you waste sitting at Starbucks going over your notes, trying to decide what you're going to do that day? How much time do you spend preparing for and attending sales meetings? And the big one for many: How much time do you spend grousing and complaining with other salespeople in your office?

Brian Tracy in his small book, *Be a Sales Superstar: 21 Great Ways to Sell More, Faster, Easier in Tough Markets*, cites a university study that revealed the average salesperson only works one week a month, whereas the superstars worked on average three weeks a month. How can this be since every salesperson you know is working all month, every month? It's all in the definition of work. In the study, "work" is defined as doing any one of the three things that make salespeople money—finding prospects, selling them, or working on completing their orders. Anything else the salesperson does is "busy work," because it isn't directly responsible for earning them a living.

Based on that definition, the study found the average salesperson spends two hours a day on activities that generate income. At two hours per day, five days a week, that works out to about one week a month.

On the other hand, top producers work six hours per day on revenue generating tasks. Is it any wonder they earn significantly more than the average salesperson? They're working three times harder!

Look at the bullet points above. How many of those tasks actually fit within the definition of "work" as defined in that study? Only four of the nine tasks meet that definition: Finding prospects through marketing and lead generation; meeting with clients and prospects; working on customer orders; and prospect and client follow-up communication. All the rest are non-income producing tasks, yet that's how most salespeople spend their time.

If you want to put your career on the fast track, decide how much time you're willing to commit to your career and establish a firm schedule you can (and will) live with. Once established, everyone should be aware of it; let people know exactly when you are available and open for business.

When constructing your schedule, take into consideration your commitments—personal and business. If your commitment is 48 hours per week, construct a schedule that takes into account the networking meeting on Tuesday night that you attend, as well as your son's baseball games every Thursday at 4:30. Schedule your vacations and days off and stick to them, because once you've published your schedule, your business is committed to those hours.

Nothing short of an emergency should shut your business down during your open hours. Invited to a game you're dying to attend? If it doesn't include a prospect or client, you can't go if it conflicts with your open hours. Feel like playing golf? You'd better be able to take a prospect or client—otherwise; it's out of the question. Need a new suit and you have an appointment over by the mall? Too bad. Go during your off hours.

Disciplining Your Moneymaking Time

Establishing your business hours is a necessary task that will help you discipline yourself. However, unless you go beyond simply establishing your business hours, you still won't generate the results you want. You have to take a further step and schedule concrete moneymaking hours within your schedule.

Moneymaking hours are those hours where you do nothing but concentrate on the three things that put money in your pocket— prospecting, selling, and taking care of clients.

You should schedule a *minimum* of 30 hours per week for those tasks—six hours a day, five days a week, on average. Depending on the schedule you establish and the primary selling hours for your business, those may end up being five hours, six days a week, or seven hours, four days a week. Whatever the schedule, it is etched in stone. Absolutely nothing save emergencies takes precedence during those times.

However, before you begin scheduling, let's define those tasks— what they are and what they aren't.

Prospecting during these times will consist of actually hunting for new prospects, not designing fliers, constructing call lists, researching prospects, writing direct mail pieces, or any other pre-prospecting activity. You are not preparing for the hunt; you are hunting.

That means if you are going to cold call, you have the list in front of you. You've done the prospect research beforehand. You do nothing but dial the phone and talk to prospects. Nothing else counts.

Making presentations and selling is just that. It doesn't include the prep time, travel time, or waiting in the client's lobby. Selling time is time spent in front of a prospect turning them into a client. It does, however, include your follow-up meetings, phone calls, and other communication.

Working on a client's file is just that: Any activity that gets the client's purchase completed. Filling out forms, communicating problems or issues to the client, providing support information, and the like are all legitimate client activities that put money in your pocket. If your activity advances the client's purchase, it qualifies—unless it can be and should be done by someone else. Helping the clerical staff or customer service just to give them a hand doesn't qualify. Mundane customer service activities are to be done by those who have that specific responsibility. You become involved in those activities only when the situation dictates action must be taken now and for some reason you cannot trust it will be done in a timely fashion by anyone else.

You'll need discipline and commitment to spend a full 30 hours a week pursing those three tasks. You probably will find that to free yourself for 30 hours doing those tasks, you will have to schedule considerably more than 30 hours. You must consider travel and prep work, plus interruptions and minor emergencies.

However, if you've scheduled a 48-hour week—eight hours, six days a week, you will have three hours each day for the necessary busy work. On the other hand, you may discover you have to dedicate more time to your career than you had anticipated, at least at first.

Becoming successful at sales isn't easy. You need skill, commitment, and dedication. What are you willing to commit to your success?

One more thing: Your published hours are not the only hours you're open. Prospects and clients don't always need you when it is convenient for you. You'll find you have to work outside your established hours from time-to-time. The good news is, these extra hours usually entail moneymaking activities.

Create and Publish Your Business Hours

Determine what time commitments you can and will make to your career. Consider your commitments outside of work and how to balance your career with your personal life, and then construct your company's business hours. Then, taking into consideration your time requirements within your business, schedule your moneymaking hours. Once you have completed the schedule, including your vacations and days off, publish it to your prospects and everyone else who needs to know what hours you are open. Then stick to it.

Disciplining Your Money

In addition to determining how much time you're willing to commit to your career, you have to determine how much money you're willing to commit. Although this is a sore spot with many salespeople, you will find it almost impossible to succeed in sales without investing money for training and personal marketing.

Again, keep in mind that you're not an employee in the traditional sense of the word. You are not like the secretary, engineer, accountant, or any other person in your company who are limited by their salaries. You are the owner of a company with only one client—the company you sell for today.

Consequently, don't think in terms of investing money to help that company. Rather, understand you are investing in *your* company, not your "client" company. You are investing in your training to become a better salesperson for your future, not for the benefit of your client. You are investing in marketing to market yourself, not your client company.

You're investing in yourself for yourself. You'll take the training you invest in everywhere you go; it doesn't stay with your current employer. You'll take the contacts you make and the reputation you develop everywhere you go. And if you've done a great job of marketing yourself, you'll take clients and prospects with you when you leave.

You are simply leasing yourself to your employer, along with the skills, experience and knowledge you have gained from the training, plus your prospect list and your clients. When you move, you take the business you have worked hard to build with you.

Obviously, this is not a popular notion with companies. They see things from a much different perspective. Nevertheless, we're not dealing with perspectives or the niceties of business; we're dealing with the reality of building a superstar sales business and superstars don't work for companies—they may lease themselves to a company, but when they leave, they take it all with them.

With that understanding of what you're investing in, you must take careful inventory of your financial situation and determine what you're willing to do. That doesn't mean what you can *afford* to invest—it means what you're willing to commit to an investment in yourself.

That number will be different for every salesperson, but you must make a commitment and then stick to it.

Training: Training is easier to deal with from an investment point-of-view. Thousands of sales and marketing articles are available on the Internet—all free for the taking. Sites such as the following contain excellent tools:

- www.topsalesexperts.com
- www.salesgravy.com
- www.eyeonsales.com
- www.salespractice.com
- www.marketingprofs.com
- www.salesdog.com

Many top sales trainers post articles on their websites and some offer free tele-seminars. Of course the tele-seminar is typically used to push the trainer's book, CD, or DVD, but many of these free seminars are valuable in themselves. However, even products you must pay for aren't expensive. A typical sales book costs less than $20, including shipping.

The CDs and DVDs you need will cost $20 to $90 for a single CD and up to several hundred dollars for sets. Plan on listening to (or reading) each product several times, not just once. Tele-seminars and webinars cost $39 to $199. Not only does the seminar allow you to hear instructions from the trainer, you're able to ask questions and receive answers on the spot.

Many industry associations offer great training opportunities for only the cost of membership. Even the most cash strapped salesperson can get a top-notch year's worth of training for less than $20 per month. By combining free articles, online sales forums and free tele-seminars with the purchase of one book or CD a month, even the poorest salesperson can afford hundreds of hours of first-class training.

If you have more than just a few dollars a month to invest in training, you can get the best of the best for only a couple hundred dollars per month; probably less than a $2,400 per year.

In addition, if you're serious about building your personal business and have the funds, consider hiring a personal sales coach. This is one of the most cost effective moves you'll ever make. Yes, coaches aren't cheap. But with the right coach, your business can go places you only dreamed of—and in a relatively short time.

If you aren't getting the training you need, it's either because you haven't tried to find it or you're waiting for your company to step up and do something. Key 9 discusses in detail how and where to find training that meets your needs and how to determine which books, CDs, seminars, and other training materials to invest in.

Marketing: This is a more challenging aspect of sales. How will you generate the business you need? The marketing channels and methods you choose may require a sizeable investment every month.

Key 4 deals with choosing the marketing channels you wish to target, while Key 5 discusses how to select effective ways to penetrate the market. The investment you're willing and able to make helps determine your marketing methods. Some methods don't cost much (cold calling, for example), while others are expensive (direct mail). It makes no sense to decide you're going to establish a direct mail campaign if your marketing budget is $50 per month.

You won't be able to make a decision about marketing methods until you settle on a budget. You need to know what you have to spend before you can decide how to spend it. The expenses are always more than you anticipate. Consider these typical marketing expenses:

- Business cards
- Stationary

- Postage

- Gas

- Phone

- Cell phone

- Brochures

- Fliers

- Prospect and client lunches

- Meeting prospects and clients for coffee

These are basic expenses for most salespeople. Eliminate any of the above your company provides, which might include business cards, copying (filers), brochures, stationary and postage. That leaves your cell phone, gas, business lunches, and coffee meetings with prospects and clients. Let's assume you use two tanks of gas a month (frugal you!). You've just spent $100 for gas. Cell phone? Probably at least $60 a month—and possibly much more. One business lunch. That's another $35. Two prospect coffee meetings. Another $20. You've already spent $215 for the month and you haven't even done anything except meet three prospects or clients. The average outside salesperson can probably double that just for starters. And if your company doesn't pay for copies and postage, triple that to $600 per month just to be in business.

Want a personal brochure? Figure that in.

Need to take more than one prospect or client to lunch? Add dollars to your personal marketing account.

Want to use networking as a primary marketing method? Add in the cost.

Want to work within various associations and organizations? Add the cost of membership and the price of individual events.

Want a direct mail campaign? Add more money.

Want to market via the Internet? Add dollars.

Want to spend time at the restaurants and places your prospects hang out? Yep, add more money to your budget.

As you can see, the dollars quickly add up, and without a definite plan of action, you'll end up going way over your budget.

Making Your Commitment: The time has come to commit. Set out your personal budget and find areas where you can sacrifice for your business. This is such an important part of both your business and personal life that you must get agreement from your whole family, because they may need to make sacrifices.

How much should you commit? A good rule of thumb is 3% of your income for personal training and 10% for marketing.

Ouch!

If your income is say, $3,500 per month, your training commitment is $105 dollars per month and your marketing is $350. Yes, that can hurt. However, it barely covers the necessities of doing your job.

If your income is $5,000, your training budget is $150 and marketing is $500. Again, you don't have any excess dollars in your marketing budget. You'll be squeezing each penny to make it work. No extravagant direct mail campaigns in your marketing plan. No two-martini client lunches for you. No taking your best client to the ballgame.

If you're earning $200,000 per year, you're monthly marketing budget is still only $1,666 per month. That doesn't go nearly as far as you may think.

Remember, you're running your own business. You're creating your future. You are building a lasting base on which your life's income will be based. What you invest now will be making you money for years to come.

If you must sacrifice anywhere, sacrifice in the dollars you commit to your training, but don't sacrifice training. In Key 9 we will discuss where and how to find great training at little or no cost. Even so, remember that if you must settle for free training, you have to take what you can get—which may not be exactly what you need.

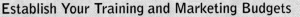

Establish Your Training and Marketing Budgets

Gather your family and carefully go over your budget. Explain the importance of the sacrifices they may have to make and describe the eventual payoff. Then establish both training and marketing budgets—and adhere to them religiously. Your budgets should be a dollar amount, not a percentage. As your income increases, increase your dollar commitment.

Summary

You've begun to make the commitments and decisions that will change your career. At this point, you should have established formal working hours and scheduled within those hours a minimum of 30 hours per week for direct moneymaking tasks. In addition, you should have your vacations and days off scheduled. This calendar should be distributed to clients and co-workers.

Each day you should have a clear idea of exactly how you will spend your time. Undoubtedly, you will encounter many intrusions, at least at first. Other salespeople in your office will want to drop by and waste your time. You'll have to explain politely that your work time is work time. You'll be tempted to take that two-hour lunch with the rest of the gang. You will be tempted to stop by the mall, since you're already out there. You will be tempted to leave early. You will be tempted to stay in bed just a little longer. You will be tempted not to make cold calls or attend the networking event—"just today."

Temptations will be around you like mine fields. Ignoring them isn't easy, but what you do now will dictate what happens in the months to come. That two-hour lunch can easily become a habit. Giving into the temptation not to make the calls today makes it easier to goof off tomorrow. Staying in bed a little longer this morning will turn into staying in bed later tomorrow, and even later the next morning.

Yet, in the same manner, making calls today makes tomorrow's work easier. Getting up on time today makes it easier to rise on time tomorrow. Learning good habits is as easy as learning bad ones, but lazy habits lead downhill, while good work habits will launch your career to new heights.

You'll need discipline and dedication to institute your schedule. You'll need to develop a new way of looking at your sales business and a new way of thinking. Key 12 will help you develop the mindset you need to reach the top. And that mindset must be accompanied by a structure that allows it to work. Structure is necessary to every business, yet, salespeople are notorious for lacking structure.

Some of your associates may laugh at you for keeping a rigid schedule. They may be put off by your new attitude, your intense focus on work, and your absence at the bitching sessions. Accept this for what it is—lack of understanding.

At this point, you should know your training and marketing budgets. You may not know exactly where the dollars will be spent, but you know how much you have to spend. Your job now is to determine the most effective ways to spend those dollars. You'll do this after you decide which marketing channels you're most suited for and how you will penetrate them. That's your next step.

Key 4: Finding Your Place in the Marketplace

When the product is right, you don't have to be a great marketer.
— **Lee Iacocca**

You may be able to sell ice cubes to Eskimos, but isn't there an easier way to make a living? One of the joys of selling is knowing you aren't one of the crowd; you've created a special niche in the market where you're a superstar.

Every salesperson dreams of being "the" expert in their field. We dream of having prospects seek us out because of our reputation and image. We envision ourselves as so busy (read *important*) that all we do is sign contracts and take an occasional celebrity client to dinner. Of course, we leave the detail work to our underlings.

Oh, what a fantasy! The scenario above makes a great dream, but it will never be a reality for the masses of salespeople, because they never put in the work to make it happen. However, that dream (in a less idealized form) is reality for thousands of sales superstars throughout the world.

What great secret allowed them to build such a business? Were they just lucky, or did they do something different?

Their great secret really isn't much of a secret at all. The superstars conquered the fear of focusing on a narrow segment of the marketplace. Instead of trying to be all things to all people, they made the conscious decision to focus their efforts on one or two niches and to become an expert for that segment of the market.

The typical salesperson's goal is to market with a broad brush. When asked by a prospect, "What's your specialty," their answer, in essence, is, "What do you want it to be? Tell me what you want and that's what I am."

It seems logical that you can attract more business by covering the entire marketplace. Salespeople take their marketing cues from the marketing they see most often. They try to emulate GM, Merrill Lynch, Nike, and other household names.

GM doesn't go after a small segment of the auto buying market. If you're in the market for a car, GM wants you. If you're looking for any type of athletic shoes, Nike wants you to buy theirs. If you are looking to invest, Merrill Lynch has the product for you.

Salespeople view their business the same way. They figure you want to finance or refinance a home, they should offer you every product under the sun. If you plan to buy a home, they can show any home that's on the market. These generalist salespeople fail to understand a few basic differences between themselves and GM. GM has millions of dollars to invest in advertising and marketing. GM has different units that focus on different segments of the market. GM spends more on niche marketing than on general marketing.

Just because you can compete with a huge corporation like GM on breadth of product doesn't mean you can compete with them on breadth of market—unless you can afford to stand toe-to-toe in the marketing battle.

In addition, you have other serious competitors besides national corporations. Every area of the country has local and regional firms entrenched in the market. Compared to a single salesperson, these smaller companies are gargantuan in terms of marketing reach and budget. Now, take it another step lower. Each of the national and regional companies has individual salespeople on the street fighting for customers. Each of them has their own mini marketing budget that's equal to or greater than yours.

The good news is, you aren't actually competing with the companies themselves, but with their salespeople—and you're on an equal footing with these men and woman. The guy who's selling GM, Honda, and Kia products for the biggest dealership in the region has to prospect for customers just as you are. The Merrill Lynch financial advisor is just as desperate for prospects as you are. The Countrywide loan officer is scraping to find loans just like you are. These are all big companies, but their individual salespeople compete on your level. Individual salespeople make the majority of the sales, not the company name.

Furthermore, these folks are probably making the same mistake you're making—trying to cast a broad net to attract as many clients as possible, believing bigger is better. Those salespeople use the same marketing methods you use. They go to the same events. They use the same worn-out phrases and sell more or less the same products. Their prices are similar. They're cold calling the same people you are, and they buy the same leads. They also have the same disappointing results.

You are lost in the crowd, a faceless salesperson in a sea of faceless salespeople, all trying to sell the same thing, to the same people, in the same way.

Is it any wonder selling is a tough business?

Of course, you've been told to memorize your own Unique Selling Proposition. The problem is every other person who's out there selling your product or service has his own variation of the same USP.

You're encouraged to uncover and solve the prospect's problems. But often you don't know enough about the prospect's industry and business to come up with anything other than a standard solution.

You're encouraged to attend Chamber of Commerce networking events, only find that half the attendees are your competitors and the other half are salespeople from other industries haunting the halls for live prospects. If they had a speaker, it could be a sales training seminar.

Nevertheless, there is a solution.

Become what your competition isn't. Become an expert in one or two smaller segments of the market and then throw all of your marketing, prospecting and sales efforts into those niches.

Yes, salespeople have a fear of narrowing their sights to focus on one segment of the market. What about the mass of potential prospects they'll miss? What about the thousands of sales that will walk right past them?

Oh, right, they weren't getting those sales in the first place, were they?

Instead of worrying about all the thousands of sales you could be missing (that you're not getting anyway), why not focus on becoming a real expert for a small segment of the market? Instead of being a faceless salesperson in a crowd, you can be the expert. That's the advantage of specializing.

By doing so, you can become intimately familiar with the needs and problems of companies and clients within your specialty area. Specialization gives you the opportunity to become a part of their exclusive group.

If you're selling to companies, you should subscribe to their industry publications, attend industry meetings, join their associations, meet and mingle with the industry leaders, and develop relationships within companies. You learn about their needs and problems, where they're hoping to go, new products and markets, and up and coming companies and individuals. In other words, you become part of the industry. You're no longer an outsider looking for a potential sale. Instead, you're involved with the industry: a trusted supplier who knows how to solve unique problems.

One of the secrets of niche marketing is the perception that you understand their issues because you specialize in that industry and realize how unique their problems are. People within every industry believe their problems and issues (and thus the solutions to those problems) are unique. Naturally, they want to work with someone who really understands their situation.

In reality, few problems and issues are unique to a particular industry or company. However, people tend to think their problems are special. By focusing on one segment of the market, you can take advantage of the perception that they are unique and need someone who understands.

Niche marketing also helps you stretch your limited marketing budget. Rather than trying to get your message out on a grand scale, you can concentrate your dollars on a more focused area. If you're like most salespeople you still won't have enough funds to do everything, but you can make those dollars work harder for you.

How do you find a niche?

You can't just wake up one morning and decide to concentrate on selling SUV's to families with three or more kids within a fifteen-mile radius of your dealership. Do you know if the market is large enough to meet your needs—that is, enough families who meet your criteria within your geographic area? Does the typical family have enough income to afford your SUV's? Are SUV's a primary product for your target families? Will you be able to isolate this group and reach them?

Perhaps your gut instinct says that SUV's are a more likely purchase for your target audience than, say, a two-seat sports car. But how do you know these families aren't buying minivans?

You might be able to look around at the neighborhoods close to the dealership and see kids everywhere. But do you know the average number of kids per family? Do you know the average income per family?

Finding your niche requires serious research. You must take a long, hard look at your market and find areas where you can become an expert in addressing "unique" problems. You'll need to answer a number of questions such as:

- What mini-markets make up the big market for your product or service? For instance, if you sell to residential builders, you would locate tract builders, semi-custom homebuilders, custom homebuilders, apartment builders, condominium builders, town home builders, remodelers with various specialties, plus other residential builders with even narrower specialties. If you sell business insurance, you'll find hundreds of mini markets, such as small companies, mid-size companies, large companies, multi-national companies, food stores, retail stores, construction companies, and trucking firms. The list could go on and on.

- Do you already have a head start in specialization? Do you have a group of clients who can become the core of your niche?

- Is the segment you're considering large enough to support your efforts? It can't be too large; yet, it can't be too small either.

- How well do your products and services fit the niche? The better you can fit your products and services, the easier to penetrate the market

- Can you join a local organization or association within your niche?

- Will you be able to isolate your niche group and obtain information about the members?

- Is the niche you're looking at already dominated by other salespeople or companies?

- Who are your primary competitors within this segment?

- What competitive advantages do you have for this segment?

- How many prospective customers are within your geographic area?

- What are the historical sales figures within your industry for sales to your target market in this geographic area?

- Do you believe you can position yourself within the target market within a reasonable period?

These can be tough questions to answer. Some may not be answerable with verifiable data, leaving you to have to make your best guess. Before you jump into a niche, do your homework. The better your research, the more likely you will make a prosperous decision.

Fortunately, you do have research tools at your disposal.

A natural place to begin your research is through your industry association and the target market's association. You'll be able to locate an association for almost any geographic, demographic, and industry segment you can imagine. You can find an extensive list of associations and organizations at www.businessresearchdatabase. com/html/associations.html.

- Association websites contain a wealth of information, such as:
- Membership lists
- Links to local chapters
- White papers and news releases about industry problems, issues and opportunities
- Industry historical sales and economic data, as well as economic forecasts for the industry
- Information about major players within the industry
- New and innovative products and services offered by the industry

- Upcoming local and national meetings, plus networking opportunities

- State, regional and national conferences and conventions—including major session topics (these are usually hot topics within the industry)

- Which, if any, of your competitors are sponsors of the organization—and any sponsorship opportunities that are available

- How to become an associate member

- What publications the association sponsors

The information and data on most association websites will help you decide if that segment is an appropriate niche market for you—and how you'll approach this market to sell your products and services. If the association doesn't give economic data and forecasts for the industry, the U.S. Government Census Bureau maintains an extensive database of recent economic data, by industry, at: http://www.census.gov/cir/www/.

If you're targeting a group of consumers rather than businesses, you will need demographic information for your geographic area. A good place to start is the ERSI, a geographic information systems company, website: http://www.esri.com/data/community_data/community-tapestry/index.html. Type in the zip code of your areas for a report listing basic demographics of the zip code, including average household income, age, home value, and more. This information is free, and you can get more detailed reports for a fee.

The latest U.S. Census results provide an excellent tool for market assessment. You can find complete census data at http://www.census.gov/. This website contains everything you ever wanted to know about your geographic area—just keep in mind the material is dated material—but still useful.

To research a market segment containing small companies, begin with Bizstats http://www.bizstats.com/. The Bizstats tool lets you research the average profitability of small business groups. For example, if you're targeting day care centers, the Bizstat tool will show you the average profit margin for a day care center. The same information is available for almost any other business.

In addition to the sites above, you should subscribe to publications for the market segment you're targeting. Magazines, email updates, blogs, and articles will help you stay up to date on important news, personalities, and innovations. At www.businessresearchdatabase.com/html/publications.html you will find several hundred industry and market segment specific publications, most of which have free subscriptions.

You'll find the Internet is an almost endless source of information as you research the niche you're examining.

Research Potential Niche Markets

List several potential niche markets you think might be appropriate for targeting and then take the time and invest the energy to research each thoroughly. Narrow you potential markets down according to size, potential sales volume, and the marketing advantages you believe you can bring to the market.

What if you find that one or two companies dominate your desired niche? Investigate those companies and see if you can find weaknesses. Do they have issues with their image, reputation, products, delivery, or service? Is there a marketing or product advantage you can bring to the marketplace? Are these companies ignoring sub-markets or geographic areas within the target market?

In niche marketing, you must make sure you can sufficiently penetrate your market within a reasonable period of time. How do you determine this? You'll have to use your best judgement, keeping in mind that the longer your sales cycle, the longer it will take to make adjustments or to reevaluate your marketing plan.

If your sales cycle is typically eight to nine months, you'll be many months into your marketing campaign before you can gather enough data to determine whether the niche is viable, or your marketing plan is producing the results you want. If you have a relatively short sales cycle (three months, for example), you can get quick feedback on your niche and marketing plan.

No matter the length of your sales cycle, don't allow yourself to become so enthused about your new niche that you abandon your other marketing channels until you have established yourself within your niche. Niche marketing can open tremendous new avenues and opportunities. However, like anything else, it takes time. If you abandon your current channels too early, you face the real possibility of starving before you even have the chance to realize the benefits of niche marketing.

Find your niche—and then enter it with a well defined plan of attack that allows for gradually moving your sales business from its current shotgun approach to a single, highly focused approach.

Summary

By now you should have taken the first steps to becoming a dominating force in your new niche market. You've moved another step closer to becoming a superstar.

You should have completed your niche market research and have one or two market segments you will target, with the intent of developing them into your core business.

If you haven't taken the time to research your intended niches, do so now. Don't march blindly into niche marketing. Finding and exploiting the right niche can send your business to new heights. Likewise, selecting the wrong niche because you didn't spend the time and energy researching it can just as quickly lead to disaster.

Andrew Failed to Research: Andrew is a successful mortgage loan officer who has been in the business for about four years. He lives in a mid-size city in the Southwest. During his first years in the mortgage business, he didn't target a particular market segment. Instead, like most salespeople, he looked for business from anyone who needed a mortgage or could refer him to someone who might.

In his second year, Andrew was faced with his first VA mortgage. Several loan officers and processors in his company warned him that VA loans were difficult to do and advised him to pass on the loan. Rather than pass up a commission, Andrew tackled the loan. His experience with the VA loan didn't reflect the warnings he received from his co-workers. He found the loan more detailed than what he was used to, but figured since he had now been through the process, it wasn't so bad. He also appreciated the fact that his commission on the loan was well above his average.

Over the next year, Andrew closed four more VA loans. Each new loan was easier than the last and they were all profitable. He thought he'd found his niche. After all, he was now the VA loan "expert" in his small brokerage company.

He was also getting dissatisfied with his employer because he felt the commission spit was too low. He resented the fact his employer gave little aid in terms of marketing or lead generation. And, besides, the mortgage industry was hot.

Andrew decided to open his own brokerage company and concentrate on what he believed was an underserved niche— military veterans. He rented a small office and signed a few contracts with wholesale lenders, including one he could send VA loans through once he completed his application and paid the fee, which he did immediately.

Andrew then struck out to market VA loans in every corner of his area where he could find vets looking to purchase a home or refinance their VA loans. He haunted the VFW posts, took out ads in the local newspapers, plastered the area with filers, and bought lists of VA homeowners.

Unfortunately, he discovered many of his assumptions were wrong. Unlike the other loan officers in his company, many loan officers working for other companies were not afraid of originating VA loans. The competition was worse than he'd imagined.

In addition, he discovered two large companies specialized in VA loans also—and they both had call centers that were constantly calling vets, seeking to help them refinance their loans.

Then there were the lists of vets he purchased. Too many out dated addresses and phone numbers. Too many other loan officers buying the same names.

Worse, he lived in a city dominated by a university that attracted a large population of arts and crafts people. The huge population of veterans he had expected wasn't there. In fact, veterans constituted only a small percentage of the population.

Too much competition chasing too few prospects.

Andrew might have established himself in his niche if he had the time and resources to persevere. Unfortunately, he didn't. What was supposed to be a killer niche turned out to be a killer, period.

He closed his office. He's still a loan officer, but with another broker; again looking for anyone seeking any kind of home financing.

Andrew jumped into this new venture without doing his homework to explore the niche to see if his idea was viable. It wasn't—at least not within his timeframe. Moreover, by the time he realized his mistake his funds were too depleted to sustain him while he changed direction.

Andrew's second mistake was entering his new niche headfirst. He didn't give himself an opportunity to build his niche. Instead, he bet everything on the assumption that the niche was right, he could penetrate it, and build a positive cash flow in short order.

Unfortunately, for Andrew the story doesn't end here. While he was off trying to create a niche for himself, he neglected his old referral sources and they found new loan officers to work with. When Andrew had to give up and join another company, he tried to reestablish his old relationships. That didn't happen. He had abandoned the relationship once, and they weren't going to give him the same opportunity again. He is now trying to rebuild his modest practice from scratch—but in a much slower mortgage environment.

Niche marketing can make your business. It is a Key to becoming a superstar. Just know exactly what you're facing, exactly how you will penetrate your new niche, and give yourself ample time to create a base within the niche before you abandon your existing business avenues.

Additional Resources

You'll find additional articles on niche marketing at www.thetwelvekeys.com/html/niche.html, as well as links to additional sites where you can research your intended niche. The information in this Key is basic. Remember, the more you know about your intended niche, the more informed your decision. Knowledge gives you the information to formulate a plan and crack your niche quickly and successfully.

Part of becoming a superstar is acting and thinking like a superstar. One of the common denominators of superstars is making well thought-out decisions based on information, not hope. Take advantage of the information resources you found in this Key and on the website.

Key 5: Aligning Your Strengths to Your Marketing Methods

*The aim of marketing is to know the customer
so well the product or service fits and sells itself.*
— **Peter Drucker**

$\mathcal{W}$elcome to the realm where the real superstars shine. Prospecting and marketing are the death of most salespeople, but in these areas superstars excel.

For our purposes, marketing will include all methods, techniques, and strategies that help you get the word out and find new prospects. To simplify our discussion, I will mix pure marketing with prospecting and public relations, since that's how most salespeople use the term (with apologies to marketing and PR professionals).

If you're new or relatively new to your sales position, how can you level the playing field with your more established competition? If you're already established, how will you take your business to the next level? If you're a big producer and you want to move your business beyond its current geographic and demographic model, how will you expand your influence and reach?

Prospecting and lead generation are the biggest problems any business faces. It doesn't matter whether we're talking about WalMart, Microsoft, IBM, a network engineering company, an individual realtor, an attorney, a financial planner, a clothing store, a restaurant, or a telecommunications consulting firm;

finding new sources of revenue—new business—is the lifeblood of every business.

The problem is, in a world where most salespeople in a given industry offer similar products and services, along with similar prices and customer service, how in the world do you stand out from the crowd?

If you don't stand out, you can't become a superstar. If you're just another salesperson trying to sell the same stuff to the same people in the same old way, you'll be swimming in a sea of faceless salespeople, scrambling for the crumbs left by the superstars.

"Whoa," you say. "Where do you get the idea that most salespeople have the same products, the same pricing, and the same customer service? That's simply not true."

Well, I think you're wrong. Almost everyone claims to have the best price or at least the best value. Many claim unique products or services. Everyone promises the best customer service.

Shop around in any field. Call 30 of your competitors this week. Ninety percent of them will be within a few percentage points of each other on price. Call again next week and you'll get the same results—except more than likely the company that offered the lowest prices this week probably won't be the low price leader next week.

Furthermore, if you do find a way to lower your price below the competition and maintain quality, how long will it be before your competition finds a way to go one better? A week? A month? A quarter?

Products and services? Hit the grocery store—every store carries the same products. Call a realtor—they sell the same houses. Call a mortgage company—they all have the same products. Call a software company that sells client relationship management software—they all claim their products do the much same thing, but their product does it better, maybe with an extra bell or whistle. Call a divorce attorney—they all do divorces. Call an investment broker: same stocks, bonds, and mutual funds, same, same, same. Different money managers? Depending on the company you call, that's true. But they all claim to be the best. Go to twenty different Honda dealers, Toyota dealers, Ford dealers, Hummer dealers, Buick dealers. Same cars. Same colors. Same options. Looking to get your network fully integrated and humming perfectly? Call a dozen network-engineering companies. They all have the best solution and give the best value.

If you do manage to develop a unique product or service, how long before your competition takes your idea and improves on it? A week? A month? A quarter?

What about customer service? This is even worse than price and product. Every company claims to have the best customer service. Yet, one of the best selling categories of business books is about—customer service. Write a customer service book and it will sell like crazy. Why? Because everyone wants to figure out how to have the great customer service they already claim to have.

Nevertheless, let's assume you do institute superior customer service. How long before a competitor discovers how to steal your customer service methods and make them even better? A week? A month? A quarter?

A few—very, very few—companies always manage to maintain the lowest price or innovate products and services to stay one step ahead. Or perhaps they're known for the best customer service in their industry. These models are out there. But I'm willing to bet you don't work for one of them.

Many of you won't appreciate the above statements. I can hear you screaming, "We're different!"

I doubt it.

I'm not trying to offend you. I'm being realistic. Hanging your hat on something that isn't true can be dangerous. Plus, even the few companies that manage to lead the pack in price, innovations, or customer service, are bound to slip at some point.

You know what's worse? Not only can't you differentiate yourself on price, product, or customer service, everyone else has the exact same marketing methods and messages that you're using.

Again, you are a faceless salesperson in a sea of faceless salespeople selling the same products at the same price, using the same methods to reach the same prospects with the same message.

Don't believe me? Ask any realtor how many mortgage loan officers they get calls from each week. Realtors who've only been in the business 60 days can give the spiel for the loan officer. Alternatively, ask someone selling their own home how many realtors have called since the For Sale sign went up. They can give the next realtor the whole speech. Ask someone who has a decent net worth and is not on the Do Not Call List how many financial advisors have called. They know the whole cold call by heart. Or, look at TV or print ads for the same products or services. Different words, different pictures, same message.

How in the world can a salesperson, independent professional, or small business owner stand out from the pack? Simply put, all you have to do is:

- Match the appropriate marketing methods to the marketing channel

- Match your marketing methods to your strengths (remember Key 2)

- Match your products or services to the appropriate need, want or problem

- Develop a reputation as an expert in what you do

This is a big task and not easy to do. But if you succeed, you'll set yourself apart from even the most dogged competition and give truth to Peter Drucker's quote at the beginning of this Key. It will make you a superstar.

Consider the Options

When you think of marketing, what methods come to mind? Probably the most obvious techniques, including cold calling, cold walking, media advertising, direct mail, networking, distributing fliers, buying leads, and seeking referral sources.

Each of these has its place in the marketing lexicon. However, you need to consider other methods as well. Let's examine a number of marketing and prospecting methods, and then establish a format to help you decide which will work best for your marketing channel, product, or service. Developing a marketing plan of attack requires a balance of the three, but you need to emphasize your strengths in order to overcome slight deficiencies in matching method to channel.

Cold Calling: This is one of the most popular ways to find new prospects and has been a proven way to generate new business almost as long as we've had telephones.

Cold Walking: Equally inexpensive (but less popular) is cold walking—going door to door. Salespeople employ this strategy in business-to-business and business-to-consumer sales.

Cold E-mails: Sending cold e-mails is growing in popularity with many salespeople and companies. Salespeople like cold e-mails because they believe they can cover a great deal of ground—sending out copious e-mails in a single day—without facing the personal rejection of cold calls and cold walking.

Networking: Networking is a time honored and effective prospecting method, but most salespeople fail to use this method to its fullest potential.

Direct Mail: Direct mail comes in the form of postcards, letters, brochures, and to inserts in advertising packages. For individual salespeople, an effective direct mail campaign is a costly investment. A typical direct mail piece costs from forty cents to well over a dollar. Responses are in the one percent to three and a half percent range. Moreover, this method works best with several mailings to the same people, which increases the cost.

Media Advertising: Radio, television and newspaper advertising is also expensive, especially for individual salespeople. In addition to the cost of the ad space, production costs can be costly. In a market of any real size, such an advertising campaign may cost tens of thousands of dollars.

Yellow Page advertising: Depending upon the product or service being offered, advertising in the yellow pages is often a reasonable way to seek business. But today's consumers use more than one yellow page directory, plus the Internet, making it more difficult for a salesperson or small business to determine where to invest their dollars. However, for the right product or service, the yellow pages may still be the best primary source.

The Internet: Although most companies have a presence on the Internet, it is still a minor part of most salespeople's marketing efforts, thanks to the high cost of driving traffic to a particular Internet site.

Writing Articles: Writing articles and having them published on the Internet and in traditional print publications can help establish your reputation as an expert. Internet publishing is relatively easy, because thousands of sites publish articles on almost any subject you can think of. Plus, you needn't be a professional writer to have your articles published.

Giving Speeches: Another reputation building activity is giving speeches to local business and civic groups. Making presentations to local groups gives you the opportunity to stand in front of business leaders in the role of the authority. These meetings help establish and reinforce your image and reputation as an expert while helping you get the word out to entire groups of prospects. In addition, you can raise questions your audience may not have considered and address specific issues you know they're struggling with—possibly moving them to seek more information.

Referrals: Often considered the single best marketing method in the arsenal of a salesperson, referrals are a marketing cornerstone for most superstars, no matter their product or service.

Word of Mouth Marketing: Often confused with referral selling, word of mouth marketing seeks to generate prospects by having clients, prospects, friends, family and other individuals spread your gospel for you.

Press Releases: Press releases are highly effective, yet sadly underused by salespeople, independent professionals and small businesses.

Marketing Partnerships: Partnering with one or more salespeople or companies who target the same marketing channel can increase your exposure, image, and sales within a relatively short time.

Becoming an Expert Source: Newspaper reporters, radio and television news reporters, and business magazine and freelance writers are constantly in need of expert sources for quotes, interviews, and to get industry data and information. Becoming an expert source can open tremendous doors.

Event Sponsorships: Sponsoring events and donating time or money to causes can garner both event/cause exposure, as well as public exposure through event advertising, news articles, and event coverage.

Trade Shows and Conventions: Depending upon your product or service, attending or exhibiting at a trade show or convention can generate a tremendous amount of buzz and many prospects— or you can waste a huge amount of time and money.

Indirect Marketing: Although it's a slower marketing format, volunteering to serve your community through various organizations can pay off long term by enhancing your image, reputation, and business connections within the community.

We've briefly touched on your marketing options without being too specific. You'll find a number of options hidden within each category. For instance, within the advertising option, you might consider renting billboards, and within the public speaking option, we could discuss hosting seminars for potential prospects.

The objective here is not a detailed discussion of every marketing and prospecting technique, but to present an overview of marketing methods and then, hopefully, decide how to match these broader categories to your chosen marketing channels, your particular product or service, and your specific strengths.

The general who wins makes many calculations in his temple before the battle is fought. The general who loses makes but few calculations beforehand.
— **Sun Tzu**

Matching Your Marketing Methods to Marketing Channels

A number of marketing methods can penetrate each marketing channel, while other methods fit specific channels.[11] For instance, if you market direct to consumers, exhibiting at conventions probably won't fit your marketing mix. Likewise, if you want to get in front of C-level executives in mid-size manufacturing companies, blasting away with unsolicited e-mails probably won't get you where you want to go.

Direct mail, referrals, cold calling, advertising, and several other methods will get your message directly to consumers. Your problem

---

1   For the purposes of this book, I define a marketing channel as a distinct group of people or companies you target

is choosing which methods best fit your product and service and your personal strengths.

Also consider the length of time each marketing method takes to produce results. While cold calling can produce immediate results, speaking to local business and civic groups often takes months to show a return on your time investment. Although pubic speaking may be a superior marketing tool for you long-term, do you have the time and patience to allow it to payoff?

Cost is always a major factor. Although direct mail may be an ideal way to reach your prospects, can you afford it? On the other hand, while you may detest cold calling, it may be the most effective affordable method you currently have at your disposal.

To make a rational decision about what methods to use, consider which of the above methods—or any variations thereof— will fit your chosen channels. Keep in mind; you need to examine each marketing channel independently of one another.

Let's say you're a mortgage loan officer and your chosen marketing channels are: 1) direct to consumer 2) realtors as referral sources, and 3) other mortgage companies who may have homebuyers they cannot serve because of a gap in their product line. You may use the same marketing methods for each of these three distinct marketing channels.

At this point, you aren't selecting the marketing methods you will employ for each channel. Rather, you're selecting potential methods to fit each channel. You are generating a global list of potential methods for further study.

Match Your Marketing Methods to Marketing Channels

Examine each marketing channel you have decided to target with the marketing methods you believe are appropriate for that channel. Don't try to eliminate any methods as too difficult, too costly, or for any other reason. Make a separate list of marketing methods you think are viable for each of your channels.

Matching Products/Services to Marketing Methods

Now that you've selected a group of potential marketing methods for each of the channels you intend to target, begin to narrow these methods by considering how appropriate they are for your particular product or service.

Are you selling a commoditized product or service, or are you selling something that requires a great deal of personal interaction to sell? Are you selling something that has been commoditized, but you're trying to reposition it as unique? Are you selling something that is not viewed as a commodity, but others are trying to commoditize it?

A commoditized product or service is one where price is the deciding factor instead of expertise. For example, many people view the following products as commodities and do not recognize the need for a high level of expertise: autos, furniture, lawn care, carpet cleaning, and office products. Customers often visit several furniture stores, hoping to find the loveseat they want at the cheapest price. They view a Ford as a Ford, and it makes no difference where they purchase the car. They believe one carpet cleaner is the much same as any other, except for price.

A product or service in the process of becoming commoditized is usually something where customers formerly needed guidance and some level of expertise at the point of sale. Now, companies are trying to sell this product or service based on price. The mortgage industry is a classic example: consumers no longer make decisions based on a mortgage company's reputation, stability or expertise, but strictly on interest rates and closing costs. Or, real estate, where realtors must now compete for listings with companies whose selling points are no longer expertise, marketing ability, or reputation, but price alone. Some companies offer to list a home for a commission as much as 2/3rds lower than the standard commission.

The products and services that customers view as too sophisticated or complicated for their decision alone are less price dependent, but even with these products, consumers try to find ways to turn them into commodities. An example is the investor who seeks counseling from a full-service broker. Once he believes he's pumped enough information out of the financial advisor, the customer moves to a discount broker to execute his transaction.

Business-to-business salespeople face the same issues. Certain business products and services have been commoditized or are in the process of becoming commoditized, while others are too complicated for a company to purchase without expert guidance. Yet, some companies try to turn their sophisticated purchases into a commodity purchase in order to save money.

Generally, if your product is sophisticated and your reach high within a company, you'll need to employ more sophisticated marketing methods. If you need to reach a vice president at

Microsoft, plastering her BMW with filers won't get you in the door. On the other hand, if you own a local nail saloon, fliers may work well for you.

If you have the hottest new bar in town, word of mouth marketing can generate quite a bit of traffic. However, if you're selling highly sophisticated networking solutions to Fortune 1,000 companies, you should find a more proactive way to reach prospects. Just because a marketing method can bring in business from your chosen marketing channel doesn't mean you should use that method. Because you have limited time, energy, and funds, you must focus on methods that produce the best results. In addition, you must match the image of your marketing method to your product or service. How you market reflects the value and image of your product or service. What message are you sending to potential customers if you try to sell Porsches by leaving your business card on every car in the WalMart parking lot?

Again, keep in mind that the more sophisticated the product or service, the more expertise the salesperson needs in order to change prospects into customers. Most prospects for high-ticket, sophisticated sales don't expect to be solicited through cold calling, faxing, fliers, or email ads. They believe successful salespeople for such products and services get their business in ways that are more sophisticated. Before you protest that their perception is incorrect, let me remind you that that doesn't matter. You deal with your prospect's beliefs as they are, not as you wish them to be.

> **Match Marketing Methods to Your Product/Service**
> Take the list of potential marketing methods you developed above and narrow them down to the methods that reflect the image of your product or service and which are appropriate for reaching your intended prospects.

Matching Marketing Methods to Your Strengths

The final and most difficult step is to match the marketing methods from your activities above to your personal sales strengths.

Making a match between methods and strengths requires more than saying, "I'm good at this, so I'll choose the activity that requires this strength." You'll find quite a few marketing methods that utilize the same basic strengths. For example, if you're good at building relationships, the following marketing methods may look good to you: cold calling, seeking referrals, networking, cold walking, and performing community service work. However, if one of your weaknesses is impatience, you'll need to find ways to minimize that weakness. Community service work could be a problem, since you won't see an immediate payoff for your efforts and will have to wait months, or even years, to get results. On the other hand, cold calling offers immediate feedback, something that fits well with your makeup.

Most of the marketing methods can be divided into two main categories: Those that are hot or relationship oriented, and those that are cold or impersonal.

Cold marketing methods insulate you from interaction with other people:

- Writing articles
- Direct mail
- Cold e-mail
- Fliers
- Media advertising
- Sponsoring events and making public donations
- Sending press releases
- Internet marketing

You may find it difficult to believe, but people can (and do) reach the top of the sales profession in spite of poorly developed interpersonal skills. These men and women fail when engaged in relationship-oriented sales, but they excel at using cold marketing methods. They are capable of generating prospects through cold marketing, and they have just enough interpersonal skills to close the sales. They tend to work with a short sales cycle, a commoditized product or service, and they are very successful at what they do.

Salespeople with poor interpersonal skills may also do well with short term interpersonal marketing methods, such as giving speeches and working trade shows and conventions where they are "on display" for only a short time and each individual interaction only lasts a few minutes.

Hot sales methods usually call for a salesperson with well-developed interpersonal skills. You needn't be Ms. Personality-Plus, but you need to have the ability to develop and maintain relationships over time.

Each hot method requires other strengths as well. Making public presentations requires more than the ability to relate to people; you'll need to tame the natural fear of performing before a crowd of strangers. Making community service work for you calls for a sincere commitment to the organization for which you're volunteering. Both of these methods are long-term investments that require patience as you wait for your efforts to pay off.

Balance is a difficult task for most of us. Trying to balance our strengths with our marketing methods is especially difficult when we watch the salespeople around us move ahead. The temptation to imitate someone else's success is always present. Imitating another person's methods will work *if* you have the strengths for that method. Otherwise, imitation can be a huge time waster.

Few of the marketing methods you employ can be judged over a short time. You'll need a certain amount of time to master the use of each technique. Then you need time to complete the sales cycle, and even more time to generate results. Too many salespeople expect immediate results. When nothing dramatic happens right away, they abandon their efforts and head off in another direction, constantly seeking the miracle cure for their marketing woes.

Most often, this dash to another marketing method isn't about impatience—it's about lack of confidence in their marketing decisions. Until they see positive results, most salespeople don't feel confident with the methods they've chosen. When results don't materialize as quickly as they want, they question their own wisdom and jump to another method, hoping that will be the "right" decision.

Carefully choosing your methods with an eye to your marketing channel, your product or service, and your personal strengths, will help you eliminate the stress and fear of picking methods that won't work. You can overcome the impatience and compulsion to move on to the next method. You can give yourself time and the freedom to develop your marketing methods into powerful, efficient tools.

> ### Select Your Marketing Methods Based on Your Personal Strengths
>
> Select the marketing methods that match your marketing channel, your product or service, and your personal strengths. Choose methods you believe in and are committed to developing.

Planning Your Marketing Campaign

You'll need to balance your enthusiasm for these newfound, perfectly matching marketing methods with a solid dose of reality. Suppose you find your ideal marketing mix is a combination of networking, referral generation, writing articles, and giving presentations to local business and civic groups. If your past marketing consisted of cold calling alone, then you'll experience a time gap before your new methods begin producing prospects. If you abandon your cold calling methods too quickly, you will also have a lapse in income—a potentially deadly gap.

Enthusiasm is great—but good judgment is better. Continue your existing marketing and prospecting methods until you establish your new marketing mix and it's reliably producing business.

Depending upon which marketing methods that fit your marketing channels, your product or service, and your personal strengths, you may face a complete change in your business. More than likely, you have retained some of your original marketing and prospecting methods, but you may be one of the few who decide to take a completely new approach.

Either way, you cannot jump in without serious planning.

It takes as much energy to wish as it does to plan.
— Eleanore Roosevelt

Acting without knowing where you're going, why your going there, and how you'll get there is as fruitless as no action at all—and just as grave.

Developing a comprehensive marketing plan takes time, but the plans you put in place today, if you diligently follow them, will become the habits and foundation of tomorrow's successful business.

In this plan, you should list each of your marketing channels as a separate entity, and then outline the actions you must take to penetrate that market. Also, include when those actions will be taken, how you will take them, and the anticipated results.

Leave nothing to chance. Superstars don't—and if you want to become a superstar, neither should you.

If you've selected two marketing channels—say you sell software to small to mid-size companies and you decide to focus on small manufacturers and transportation companies as your marketing channels, each will have a marketing plan segment of its own.

Within your plan for small manufactures, you will define in detail:

- your ideal prospects

- identify as many prospects as you can; these are the companies you will target

- if possible, list the decision makers within each organization

- outline how you will get to these companies, using the marketing methods you have chosen

- outline specific actions you must take within each marketing method you have chosen, along with a calendar of when those actions will be taken

- establish timelines and key dates to evaluate your progress

- set specific monthly, quarterly, semi-annual, and annual sales and income goals (see Key 6 for how to make realistic sales and income projections)

Before you move on to planning your marketing efforts within the transportation channel, you will have a complete schematic of your actions and the anticipated results of the small manufacturer segment. You'll know which small manufacturers you will approach. You'll know exactly how you will use each marketing method you chose, what actions you must perform to implement those methods, and exactly when you will perform them. You'll know exactly what you plan to sell and what your income will be. In addition, you'll know when and on what criteria you will evaluate your plan's success. The only true variable in your plan is what you plan to sell to each prospect, since at this point you don't have a full understanding of the prospect's needs. However, your plan to reach the prospect will be based on sound reasoning.

Once you have your small manufacturing leg of your marketing plan completed, perform the same exercise for the transportation leg.

In the above example, the salesperson chose two marketing channels, each with a separate calendar of events and sales and income projections. Had he chosen three marketing channels, he would have three calendars.

But working from two, three, or four calendars isn't feasible. Your last project is to integrate all the individual marketing calendars into a single master calendar—your working calendar that will include every action you've planned for the coming year, including vacations and days off. Your working calendar is a comprehensive document with actions, goals, and evaluation timelines.

Since life doesn't always go as planned, your plan isn't etched in stone. At set periods during the year, you will pause to evaluate the plan's effectiveness and make adjustments. It would be well for more marketing gurus to learn what Publilius Syrus knew two thousand years ago:

> *It is a bad plan that admits of no modification.*
> — **Publilius Syrus**

Refusing to make changes when change is called for is the bane of many a marketing department. Don't get caught in the same trap.

On occasion, you may need to abandon a channel or a marketing method. More often, adjustments are called for, not abandonment. Mixing the right methods with the right timing is not easy. Testing and experimentation will give you solid information to make well-informed decisions. The easiest way to make rational decisions is to monitor your marketing and keep accurate records. Too often salespeople implement marketing without considering how they will evaluate its effectiveness—or against what standard.

Understanding marketing metrics—the numbers used to determine the success or failure of a particular marketing strategy or to make statistically based projections—is a complicated issue and one not appropriate for evaluation here. However, if you'd like to explore the how and why of marketing metrics more thoroughly, a good starting point is Marketing NPV's website where you'll find a number of free articles and tools: www.marketingnpv.com.

How can you evaluate your marketing efforts? While constructing your plan, set out the evaluation criteria you will use when evaluating each channel and method's results. Establish minimum acceptable results for specific time periods. For example, if you're using direct mail, determine your minimum acceptable results after your second or third mailing, and then again after your fourth or fifth. If the results are acceptable, keep monitoring. If the results don't meet your minimum standards, you'll have to find out why. Is it design? Is your list too small? Are you contacting the wrong people? Is it the message?

Testing your methods by using variations is standard procedure in marketing. If you're mailing 1,500 pieces, try using two or even three variations of the piece, and then track the results. This method will produce feedback more quickly than using only one design and one message per mailing. If things aren't going well, experiment with variations on direct mail pieces, e-mails, advertising, and other marketing materials, so you can fine-tune both your message and your presentation. Before abandoning, experiment.

On the other hand, if you find your channel or marketing method was a complete bomb, then please move on. Rethink your approach. Reevaluate your possible channels and make a positive move to improve your business. Hanging on simply for the sake of hanging on, not admitting a mistake, or hoping for a miracle, won't improve your business and may even kill it.

With any marketing campaign, testing and analyzing your efforts is critical. Remember, your selling career *is* your company. Manage it like a company. You must think not only like a salesperson, but also like a CEO, a VP of marketing, and a comptroller.

Finally, once your plan is complete, buy into it completely. A halfhearted attempt to implement a marketing plan is destined to fail. If you aren't committed to your plan, then there's no sense in planning to begin with.

> *Unless commitment is made, there are*
> *only promises and hopes; but no plans.*
> **— Peter Drucker**

Construct Your Personal Marketing Plan
Construct your personal marketing plan including a complete separate leg for each marketing channel you have chosen. Create your timelines and key dates and then integrate each into your master calendar.

Summary:

You should now have:

- selected your target marketing channels

- determined your marketing methods based on your products/ services and personal strengths

- developed a complete marketing plan for each channel you have chosen

- created a comprehensive calendar for marketing, production, and evaluating dates and events

- know your evaluation criteria for each channel you target and each method you use

- have confidence in and be totally committed to executing your marketing plan

The next Key will help you make realistic sales and income projections. Therefore, be prepared to make adjustments to your marketing plan as we proceed. In fact, your marketing plan is far from complete. Not only do you need to evaluate the sales and income projections you've made so far against the process presented in the next Key, you must also integrate your client and prospect communication program (Key 8) and your personal training program (Key 9) into your plan and calendar.

Nevertheless, you should know where you're going and how you'll get there. You should target your landmarks along the way. You should be fully committed to your plan and to your success. (We will deal with the mental aspects of success commitment in Key 12).

Additional Resources

At www.thetwelvekeys.com/html/marketing.html you'll find a more detailed discussion of each marketing method, along with a number of additional resources, articles, and links to help you work through your selection of marketing methods and match them to your marketing channels and personal strengths.

Key 6: Realistic Sales and Income Projections

It's tough to make predictions, especially about the future.
— **Yogi Berra**

$\mathcal{M}$any salespeople and managers hate making sales and income projections because they believe they're just picking numbers out of the air. For most, that is the case. But for superstars this process is energizing. Their numbers are real—and they love to see numbers they know will become reality over the coming months.

Trying to project sales income for the next quarter or the coming year can be an exercise in unfounded hope if we guess at numbers and make empty projections. Hope not rooted in reality is delusional. And delusion is what many a sales career is built upon. As the old Italian proverb says, "The person who lives by hope will die by despair."

This state of delusional hope isn't where you want to be. It happens when you lack a rational way to make projections—when you don't have access to vital information. However, you can make realistic, attainable projections based upon your personal history. Unlike a big company that must use sophisticated statistical analysis, you need only understand your history in order to make realistic projections—and transform those numbers into reality.

Superstars generate realistic numbers because they know what they've done in the past and they know what they will do in the future. They base the future on their track record. They know exactly what it takes to make their projections reality. Once they make a projection, all they need do is perform the tasks the projection is based on.

You already have the information you need—you uncovered it through your diligent work in Keys 1 through 5. At this point, you know your sales history, including your production and marketing ratios; you know what channels you will target and the methods you will use to penetrate those markets; and you know how much time and money you're willing to commit to your business during the coming year.

Your projections for the coming quarter and year are based 100% on your past ratios. Even if you plan to change marketing channels or marketing methods, you will base your future sales and income projections on the reality of what you accomplished in the past.

For example, in Key 1, the financial services salesperson has a close ratio of 42.8%. Their average commission per client is $943.33. He met an average of seven new prospects per month and made an average of three sales per month.

Our analysis of this salesperson's activity indicates he hasn't been active enough to make a significant number of sales or earn the income he desires. In addition, he's having difficulty selling his more profitable products and services. Although the average sale nets a commission of about $943, the average non-sale leaves a commission of about $1,500 on the table.

If we fill in other numbers, we can follow the salesman as he makes sales and income projections for the coming year.

During his analysis, he found his close ratio when cold calling was 27.41%. He also discovered that in order to get one appointment with a prospect, he had to make 73 calls to reach eight people to get one appointment. He reached about 11% of the people he called and set appointments with 12% of the people he reached. For every 100 calls, he generated 1.3 appointments. On average, he made less than 100 cold calls per month during the pervious year. The analysis also shows he generated more appointments and sales by calling small business owners at their place of business than by calling people at home.

This salesperson also discovered he closed 50% of the prospects he met through networking. During the course of the year, he sporadically attended local Chamber of Commerce meetings and functions. He attended 11 out of 27 chamber functions, met four good prospects, and sold two of them.

While constructing the marketing plan in Keys 4 and 5, this salesperson decided he would continue marketing to the direct to consume channel, wean himself away from cold calling, and increase his networking activities.

In order to increase sales volume and income as quickly as possible, the marketing plan calls for him to continue cold calling as he works to implement other marketing methods he hopes will replace cold calling as a primary method. Consequently, he will increase his monthly cold calling activity from less than 100 cold calls per month to 800 cold calls per month—an increase of over 700 calls. Moreover, he will stop calling people at home and only call small business owners at their place of business.

Since he's eliminating residential calls and only concentrating on business owners, he anticipates an increase in both appointment and closing ratios. In addition, since he now knows he has been weak in selling the more profitable product, he will consciously focus on selling products that generate higher commissions.

The temptation while constructing the marketing plan's sales and income projections is to radically increase his cold calling numbers, based on these three factors: increased activity, focusing on business owners, and selling the most profitable products. The salesman believes he can increase his closing ratio by 20% and his commissions by at least 25%.

Yet, if he lets himself project furture sales based on unproven numbers, he's venturing into the realm of hope. He leaves reality behind. Rather than increasing his projected numbers based on the new marketing strategies, he must base his projections on the reality of past performance. Anticipating better ratios due to targeting a more specific group or earning higher commissions based on concentrating on higher commission products is an unfounded hope, not reality.

If this salesperson projects cold calling numbers based on the *belief* that his numbers will improve, his monthly cold calling projections, based on making 800 calls per month, would be:

- 10.4 appointments per month
- 3.42 sales per month
- $4,032.74 in cold call commission per month

However, if his projections are based on his actual historical ratios, he will have:

- 10.4 appointments per month
- 2.85 sales per month

- $2,689.09 in cold call commissions per month

We see a significant difference between what the salesperson hopes for and what his history says will happen. If he makes the same unrealistic adjustments to all three marketing channels he plans to use, his projected income could differ from historical income (based on actual data) by 40, 50, $60,000 or more for the year.

This salesperson is projecting a significant increase in sales and income due to increased activity, even without factoring in the anticipated increase from targeting business owners and selling more profitable products.

What happens if he does in fact see an increase in appointments due to his targeting only business owners and does in fact increase his sales of higher commission products? He sells more and makes more money. He busts the projections made based only on his past ratios—something everyone likes to do.

But what happens if the increased appointments and higher commissions he projected doesn't come to pass? Then he faces guilt, frustration, and a sense of a failure.

Projections should be based on your history, not your hope. For the salesperson above, increasing his cold calling activity eight-fold is a big step in itself and, based on his past cold calling history, should significantly increase his sales and income. However, anticipating additional income from changing his focus to business owners and selling more profitable products is based on hope, not historical data.

Likewise, if the salesperson projects a large increase in his networking commitment, these projections should be based on the additional networking commitment only, not a theoretical increase in selling products that are more profitable.

How do you make projections for a completely new type of marketing method? What if you're planning to seek referrals from people whose client base would provide good prospects for your products or services but you don't have historical data for this method?

You have four options:

1. If your new marketing method is similar to methods you already use, it's safe to extrapolate current networking numbers from one channel into your new channel, allowing for a significant ramp-up period with no sales as you build your network. For example, if you now obtain referrals from realtors whose clients need your services, you could use these numbers to approximate the income from new clients you obtain by networking with small homebuilders whose clients need your services. The more similarities between the two channels or methods, the more confidence you can have in your projections.

2. The second option is to project no sales or income. If your new channel or method doesn't relate to any of your historical methods, or if the method will require a substantial time period before results come in, then do not project sales or income from this activity. Examples of this might be community service projects, writing articles for the local newspaper, or giving speeches to local business and civic groups.

3. Some of the marketing methods, although powerful once developed, take a considerable amount of time to begin producing results. This especially applies to public relations

campaigns. It is difficult, actually impossible, to make realistic projections for these methods. Rather than viewing them as income generators, consider them adjuncts to your more immediate marketing methods. Think of them as non-income producing, but tilling the ground and planting seeds to be watered and reaped by other methods.

4. Finally, you can project sales and income performance for new channels and methods by using historical numbers from your *worst* performing channel and marketing method. By so doing, you assume your new channel or method will perform at a level no worse than your current worst performing channel and method. Be aware that even if you use worst-case numbers, you must factor in a reasonable period of non-production for the new method, since it will probably take some time to begin producing sales. If you plan to use a method that requires an excessively long ramp-up period such as writing articles, working networking through civic organizations, or giving prospect seminars, then even the worst-case numbers won't be appropriate.

What happens if you discover one or more of your channels or methods is greatly outperforming your projections? Simply revisit your plan and do another projection based on your new data. I caution you not to revise your projection until you have enough historical data to be sure your original numbers were inaccurate. Your sales and income numbers from one great quarter may be deceptive. Generally, you will need to wait longer than one month, or even one quarter, before you revise your projections.

> ### Rework Your Marketing Plan Sales and Income Projections
>
> Revisit your marketing plan and recalculate your sales and income projections based on your historical numbers. Be consistent in how you treat the new marketing channel and marketing method projections.

Summary

Assuming you've been realistic in selecting marketing channels, methods, your commitment of time and money, and the methods you use to project sales and income, you should now have a realistic, workable, and attainable plan that includes accurate sales and income projections.

If you find your projected sales and/or income fall below what you want or what you believe is attainable, you must rework the plan. If your plan doesn't allow for the sales or income you need, you need to find realistic ways to increase the numbers.

To this point, you've been creating your ideal marketing plan. You have formed your plan based on your personal strengths, your sales history, and your ideal time and money commitment. If your ideal plan doesn't take you where you want to go, it's time to make some hard decisions.

Reality is neither good nor bad, it just is.
— Arbie M Dale

Reality can be cruel, but it is what it is. What if you reevaluate your entire marketing plan and still find you can't reach your sales and income goals during the coming year? Maybe you aren't willing to invest enough time to reach your goals. Perhaps your available channels are too limited. Perhaps you need to take radical steps to improve your sales skills.

You may find you have to use the coming year as a steppingstone to position yourself for future years. If that's the case, dedicate yourself to making this year the foundation of the sales career you want for yourself. The next Key will discuss how to find and develop the selling process that fits your channels, products and strengths. In Key 9, you will construct your training schedule for the next year. Key 12 will help you develop the mindset, attitude, and mental strength to reach your goals.

Consider also that you may need to think about change. If your current position, company or product doesn't allow for you to reach your goals, maybe a change is in order. Are you not going to reach your goals because you cannot--or because your product or service, your company, or the marketing channels available to you will not let you?

If you are limited in reaching your goals because of your own deficiencies, you can correct them. Nevertheless, if you are boxed in because of something outside yourself—your product, your market, or your company, you will have to find solutions outside yourself.

Are there markets outside your immediate or traditional market you can pursue? Are there other products or services you can bring on board that will expand your market? Are there ways to overcome limitations your company has or may put on you?

If your answers are no, then maybe you are selling the wrong product or are working for the wrong company.

There is nothing wrong with well-reasoned change. Moreover, if change is in the cards, change quickly, since waiting to make a change is delaying building your business.

Key 7: Find Your Sales Process

When the only tool you own is a hammer,
every problem begins to look like a nail.
— **Abraham Maslow**

*F*inding prospects is the most difficult challenge faced by salespeople, professionals, and business owners. The inability to keep enough prospects in the pipeline drives more people out of sales than all other factors combined. Nevertheless, finding prospects isn't the only problem salespeople face.

Once you locate a prospect what do you do with him? How do you take a prospect from initial contact to client?

Most salespeople don't operate with a consistent, comprehensive process to move prospects from initial meeting to completion of sale. For the typical salesperson, selling is a series of loosely related events that, when combined, may (or may not) sell their product or service.

In fact, many sales trainers don't recognize selling as a process that can be codified. I've heard more than one sales trainer comment that they personally don't have a process and don't understand what a "sales process" is or why anyone would need it.

Yet, every salesperson has some process through which they take a prospect. Even no process is a process: It's called luck. The question isn't whether you have a process, the question is – do you have an effective, ethical, and efficient process?

Superstars have such a process. They know exactly how to move the prospects they meet from prospect to client. They know what needs to happen before it occurs, because they know exactly where they're taking each prospect and how they'll take her there. They don't operate by chance; they use a well thought-out, rational process that takes advantage of what they do well—and minimizes what they don't do well.

The scope of *SuperStar Selling* is not to present or teach you a selling process. Still, in order for you to reach superstardom, you must develop a process that:

- Allows you to use your strengths
- Effectively and repeatedly produces the results you seek
- Can be easily replicated
- Is ethical
- Matches your marketing channels
- Utilizes your marketing methods

Since the object here is not to teach a particular process, I'll lay out a few selling processes and direct you to resources where you can learn more about each. By no means am I presenting a comprehensive list of sales systems. Rather, my objective is simply to introduce several processes that demonstrate various modes that are current in the industry. These processes are all currently in use and additional information is quickly available at www.thetwelvekeys.com/html/processes.html.

I do not endorse any particular process. As you've discovered, salespeople have different strengths, marketing channels, products, and services – along with different views of how they want to conduct their sales business. Each of the processes I will present takes a different view of the role of salesperson and prospect in the sales process. They allow you to use different skills and strengths. They are all valid, but not all may be valid for you.

Furthermore, I'm sure every author cited will take exception to my description of the system he or she endorses – and my anaysis of strengths and weaknesses. Short descriptions cannot do justice to any of these processes, but examining them in depth would take far more space than we can dedicate here.

High Probability Selling: The express purpose of the High Probability Selling model is to create a mutually beneficial relationship between you and your client. Nothing new or unusual about that.

With this process, your first objective is to find only High Probability Prospects. If a prospect is not ready to buy *now*, they are of no interest to the salesperson using this model. The theory is, there are many people who want your product and service *now*, and want to work with you *now*. You can't afford to waste time and resources on people who aren't ready to purchase right away.

High Probability Selling rejects the traditional concept of "courting" prospects. The salesperson's initial job is to *disqualify* prospects as quickly as possible, leaving him with a short list of prospects who are interested in an immediate purchase.

According to the High Probability Selling model, traditional sales methods produce an adversarial relationship between salesperson and prospect. The object of High Probability Selling is to erase that adversarial relationship and replace it with a partnership where salesperson and client work as partners to resolve the client's needs.

High Probability Selling falls within the "partnership selling" paradigm and sees selling as a collaborative effort, yet still an effort that is directed and lead by the salesperson.

For more information on High Probability Selling, see *High Probability Selling: Re-invents the Selling Process* (Bookworld Services, 1997), by Jacques Werth and Nicholas E Ruben.

SPIN Selling: *SPIN Selling* (McGraw-Hill, 1988) by Neil Rackham is one of the classics in consultative selling. Although almost 20 years old, this book remains one of the best selling sales process books on the market.

SPIN is an acronym for Situation/Problem/Implication/Need-payoff. These are the four types of questions with which a SPIN salesperson engages a prospect. Produced from sales research by the Huthwaite Corporation, the process helps a prospect recognize a problem or need by asking questions that lead to solutions and an eventual resolution. Needs analysis and resolution are the heart of the SPIN process.

Rackham claims that traditional sales methods and processes may be appropriate for small dollar consumer sales, but once the solution's price tag goes past a one-time close product or service, and certainly when the price tag reaches six or seven figures, traditional selling methods are inadequate and require a more sophisticated, needs analysis approach.

You can learn more about the SPIN process from a number of White Papers published by Huthwaite at www.huthwaite.com.

Buying Facilitation: Sharon Drew Morgen has drawn on her study of consultative selling, neuro-linguistic programming, and her experience as a salesperson to develop the Buying Facilitation process.

Like the many other modern selling processes, Buying Facilitation seeks to eliminate the perceived adversarial relationship between salesperson and prospect inherent in traditional selling methods.

Rather than actively selling, a salesperson who uses Buying Facilitation prepares a path that facilitates the prospect's ability to purchase. In essence, the buyer creates his or her own purchasing experience with the salesperson as the facilitator.

More information, including information on Sharon Drew's book, *Selling with Integrity: Reinventing Sales Through Collaboration, Respect, and Serving* (Berrett-Koehler Publishing, 1997) can be found at www.newsalesparadigm.com.

Low Profile Selling: Low profile selling, advocated by Tom Hopkins, is a traditional selling method that seeks to eliminate the traditional position of the salesperson and client as adversaries. Although a traditional process, it is in-line with current sales theory with its desire to put the salesperson and prospect into a partnership rather than the more traditional seller/buyer relationship.

In his book of the same name, Hopkins presents a traditional process without the hype or high-pressure so often associated with traditional selling. Rather than traditional selling on steroids, this is traditional selling on Valium. The approach is quiet, prospect centered, and brings in some aspects of consultative selling. The title of Chapter One, "Lion or Lamb? Your Choice," gives us a glimpse into this selling method.

For additional information, consult *Low Profile Selling: Act Like a Lamb, Sell Like a Lion* (Tom Hopkins International, 1994).

Question Based Selling: In his book, *Secrets of Question Based Selling: How the Most Powerful Tool in Business Can Double Your Sales Results* (Sourcebooks, 2000), Thomas A. Freese describes a process for selling that is based more on questions than on presentations. Freese claims his system totally redefines the sales process, turning it from a confrontation between salesperson and prospect to a discovery of needs and issues, with final illumination of the prospect through targeted questioning.

Freese's method takes you from the initial contact through the sale, with emphasis on the type of questions you ask to pique a client's interest, gather information, and uncover needs.

The New Strategic Selling: Robert B. Miller and Stephen E. Heiman's, *The New Strategic Selling: The Unique Sales System Proven Successful by the World's Best Companies* (Business Plus; revised and updated edition, 2005) is the updated edition of the book originally published in 1985. This is one of the foundational books on consultative sales and the book that launched Miller Heiman's training business to worldwide fame.

Designed specifically for complex sales involving multiple decision makers, the process has been adapted in many forms by salespeople from non-complex sales industries.

The New Solution Selling: *The New Solution Selling: The Revolutionary Sales Process that is Changing the Way People Sell* (McGraw-Hill, 2003) by Keith M. Eades is an update of the original *Solution Selling* first published in 1994.

The concept behind solution selling is not to sell products or services, but to isolate problems and sell a mutually agreed upon solution to the prospect's problem. Like consultative selling, solution selling has become a buzzword employed by most companies and salespeople around the world.

Designed for use in complex, long-term sales cycle industries, The New Solution Selling process calls for identifying a complex problem and reaching a mutually agreeable solution with the prospect. The salesperson sells the solution, not products or services. Products and services become part of the infrastructure used to implement the solution.

CustomerCentric Selling: *CustomerCentric Selling* (McGraw-Hill, 2003), written by Michael Bosworth and John Holland, is a process for the long-term, complex sale (notice a pattern?) that combines the solution-based and question-based sales processes. This method emphasizes moving each prospect to his own conclusion that, of course, will require your products or services.

Bosworth is the original author of *Solution Selling,* revised by Eades into the *New Solution Selling.* Bosworth's new effort builds on his original thinking and adds several new dimensions.

However, in essence, his goal is to eliminate the need for a formal presentation through conversation and questioning, leading the sale, and allowing prospects to "find" their way themselves.

Almost all of the above processes target long-term, highly complex sales. They assume that more mundane, "normal" consumer sales don't call for the same process as a complex sale. Over the past two decades, business authors and sales trainers have focused primarily on the complex sale process, because they believe that's is where the money is—not only for the salesperson, but for them with their training programs and books.

Yet, having a process that keeps us on track, focuses the attention of both the salesperson and the prospect, and leads to a logical conclusion is just as crucial for a salesperson who sells financial services as for someone who sells a multimillion-dollar networking "solution." Consumer sales can be as complicated as complex business-to-business sales. Just ask a financial advisor who's tried to acquire a ten million dollar investment portfolio from a prospect. Sure, the process involves a single investor, but he may bring his attorney, his accountant, and several advisors to the table. Complex is complex, whether you sell business-to-business or business-to-consumer.

Whether your sales are simple or complicated, it's distressing, and potentially embarrassing for any salesperson to *become lost in the sale without knowing how to get back on track.* A comprehensive process that can be repeated in any sales situation will not only keep you on track, but also help you develop your presentation, no matter what method you use, in an effective manner.

In many ways, seling is similar to sports. Developing a series of plays – actions you think out beforehand and perfect – will generate confidence. With diligent practice, your plays will become second nature, allowing you to deviate and improvise; to address customer concerns and questions without becoming lost.

Many companies recognize the need for a structured process and over-compensate by creating canned presentations, complete with PowerPoint or flip charts and scripts their salespeople are required to use. Some companies in highly regulated industries are so fearful their salespeople will be out of compliance with industry regulations that they force their people to stick to a prescribed presentation. Others have so little confidence in the people they hire that they try to turn them into human tape recorders, replaying a "tape" the company records inside their heads. Neither of these formats is selling.

Selling is not being a parrot, regurgitating a memorized script. Selling involves understanding a prospect's situation and addressing it to satisfy a want or need. True selling calls for a human being relating with another human being through dialogue, not diatribe. However, a good dialogue requires structure—a broad, flexible outline you can adapet to each prospect's unique situation.

The process you choose is not the most crucial aspect of selling. Having confidence and a high comfort-level with the process are the most vital factors. For some salespeople that thought is a sacrilege. For others it will bring relief.

Yet, the process you select is important. In fact, your prospects may expect a particular process for the products and services you sell. Some processes are so entrenched within industries that you'll find it difficult to compete if you deviate from the norm.

Nevertheless, for most salespeople, the process should be the slave, not the master. Adopting or creating a process to highlight your strengths and diminish your weaknesses should be your goal, not finding the "perfect" process.

Virtually all the processes highlighted above rely heavily on a salesperson's ability to develop close personal relationships. Some, such as Rackham's, Eades', and the Miller/Heiman models, anticipate a long sales cycle that covers months, or even years.

Because the process is specifically designed for a long cycle, it requires a patient, persistent salesperson.

Morgen's process is excellent for salespeople who feel uncomforable with a direct, strong leadership role in the sales process. This process allows the salesperson to lead without seeming to do so. The process lends itself well to the salesperson that feels "selling" is too pushy and prefers to "go along" with the client, even though, in reality, the salesperson is still leading.

The Freese question-based model works well for salespeople who are more comfortable in a conversation instead of a formal presentation. This model doesn't eliminate presentation, but integrates it into a question-answer session instead of having questions as a prelude to the presentation. Although the process was developed for the complex sale, it works well in any selling situation and may be the perfect system for highly inquisitive salespeople.

Although most complex sale systems assume the salesperson performs at a high level of critical thinking based on selling a sophisticated product or service, these methods have been successfully adapted to less intellectually challenging sales. Don't ignore a process just because it was designed for a particular situation. All are flexible enough to work in selling situations for which they weren't originally intended.

The Hopkins system is the most adaptable for salespeople who work in consumer sales. Based on the traditional selling process, the system can be as brief and straightforward or as detailed as you want. Additionally, it aligns well with the training a typical consumer salesperson has received.

High Probability Selling conforms to the needs of the impatient, aggressive salesperson because it targets only "hot" prospects who are ready to buy now. For a salesperson who has little patience in pursuing a prospect over an extended period of time, the emphasis on "now" is not only attractive but also essential for his concentration and interest.

None of the systems are so rigid that you can't fine tune them to your needs. Each is a roadmap to a common end—a sale. And, to some extent, you can integrate multiple systems—as Bosworth and Holland have done with CustomerCentric Selling, although the integration process may prove more trouble than it's worth.

Finding your own system requires you to investigate and maybe even "try on" at least some of the methods we've considered. An eclectic system of your own is acceptable if it leads to your goal and allows you to feature your strengths without illuminating your weaknesses.

If your product or service falls within the complex sale format, you already have the attention of the sales training world. You are their primary target, with many options at your disposal.

If you don't sell within the world of the complex sale, you've been ignored by the experts when if comes to developing a comprehensive process. Nevertheless, research and investigation into the complex sale will benefit you also. The current emphasis on the customer, eliminating (or at least reducing) conflict and the adversarial role, and finding ways to turn products and services into solutions has worked its way into your world. Consequently, many of the same techniques used in the complex sale can be adapted to your sales business.

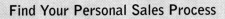

Find Your Personal Sales Process

Take time to investigate the various sales processes and try some of them on for size. Study the brief analysis of each of the systems and look into those that seem to fit you best. Finding your ideal process may take months as you study, experiment, and adapt them to your sales business.

Ellen's Process: Ellen, one of my coaching clients, consulted with me because she felt she needed more focus when dealing with prospects. Her sales presentations often didn't seem to connect with her prospects.

Her issue wasn't with understanding the products; she knew them cold. Moreover, it wasn't her ability to relate with people, because she is likeable and gets along well with people. Yet, she has problems moving prospects to a decision.

As we explored her sales process, it became clear she didn't have one. Each presentation was spontaneous—meaning disorganized. At times, she started by questioning the prospect; at other times she jumped right into her presentation.

Sometimes she skipped everything, made assumptions about the client's needs and went straight to trying to close a sale. She often spent a great deal of time establishing rapport, leaving almost no time to discuss business. During the eighteen months of her sales career she had come to dread meeting new prospects, believing she couldn't control the meeting.

In short, Ellen would become lost in the sales event and didn't know how to get back on track. Of course, she did have prospect meetings that went well. She would try to replicate those meetings during her next appointment but would inevitably get off track and be unable to find her way back.

Her company's training emphasized the need for the salesperson to maintain control of the conversation. "Only ask open-ended questions and try to ask questions that force the client to the conclusion you want him to reach. Keep the focus on the benefit you're providing. Don't let the prospect wander. Deflect objections and go back to the benefits. Always be closing."

Ellen isn't dumb, nor is she lazy. She is, however, not the least bit pushy. She is not comfortable in a leadership position. She doesn't want to take charge of situations.

The methods taught by her company are totally inappropriate for her. She isn't going to become an aggressive, lead-the-customer-where-you-want-him-to-go salesperson no matter how much training, direction, or encouragement she gets from her manager and the company trainers. Their one-size fits all training doesn't fit Ellen and cannot force her into their mold.

I had her tape record a number of her meetings with prospects and we discovered her good meetings were those where she allowed herself the freedom to discuss the prospect's situation without trying to force the conversation back on track. When she allowed herself to forget about the training and simply ask questions, she was far more successful than when she tried to force herself into a leadership role during the meeting. Yet, by focusing on questions, she *was* the leader. She controlled the situation without overtly controlling the prospect.

We practiced her questioning skills, worked her presentation into her questions and the normal conversation she had with her prospects, and turned closing into a natural culmination of the conversation. Her meetings were far more comfortable for her—and probably for her prospects. Her closing ratio more than doubled.

Ellen's experience isn't magic. She simply found a process to match her strengths. She eliminated the process she was taught, because it highlighted her weaknesses instead of catering to her strengths. She replaced it with a process that minimized her weaknesses and allowed her to do what she does well—relate to people.

Summary

Having examined your personal strengths in Key 2 and explored potential selling processes in this Key, you should now have the beginnings of a sales process that will let you focus on your strengths. Or, at the least, you'll have ideas about which processes fit you.

You should be comfortable with each of the major areas of selling, whether your chosen process is traditional, consultative, solution, customer centered, facilitating the purchase, or any other method with which you're comfortable. However you define your process, it should be your process, not someone else's.

At this point, you should know exactly how you will handle each prospect situation. You should know where your sales meeting needs to go, how you'll get there, and how you'll get back on track if the meeting goes off course.

You should be confident in your ability to meet a prospect, develop a relationship, and lead the prospect through the sales event. More importantly, you should be able to lead yourself through the sales event.

Additional Resources

For additional discussions of sales processes, including other processes, and for more resources for each, visit www.thetwelvekeys. com/html/process.html. In addition, you'll find a number of articles that deal with selling as a process.

Key 8: Developing a Communication Campaign That Advances Your Cause

It is the quality rather than the quantity that matters.
— **Seneca**

*I*f you're a sales professional, you know the importance of staying in touch with your prospects and clients and have been encouraged to do so since the first day you entered the industry. You must create and maintain a communication network.

Superstars use their communication programs in ways that go beyond the typical salesperson's techniques. Superstars understand that communicating with prospects and clients is one of the most important parts of building a relationship with each *individual.* Superstars don't just communicate; they build trust. They show each client and each prospect they honor and value his or her time. They treat each as an individual, even when sending out mass communications.

Pick up any book or listen to any CD on sales training or marketing and you'll hear the same message over and over— maintain contact. You are exhorted to send postcards, letters, emails, birthday cards, and all manner of other communication.

The communication message has been preached so often that an industry has sprung up to create postcards designed specifically for salespeople in various industries. Companies like VistaPrint, Quantum Mail, and The Personal Marketing Company will handle contact mailings for you, especially postcards. Many of these companies allow you to customize the cards with your own message and design. Unfortunately, these are still mass mailings.

Other companies, such as Send Out Cards, can help you make postcard communications highly personal. Not only can you write your own message and upload a design; you can send the cards individually, meaning each card you send is created for a specific person and contains your cursive signature. Of course, these are considerably more expensive than generic mass mailings.

Other companies entered the market by designing industry specific newsletters you can send to your mailing list on a monthly or quarterly basis. Companies such as Mostad and Christensen for accountants, Wealth Writers for the financial services industry, and Realty Times for the real estate industry hope you'll subscribe to their services to supply your newsletter. Although each company "personalizes" the newsletters for you, these are still generic, mass communications. Personalization consists of including your name, contact information, and possibly a short article written by you. Most of the content is canned.

Still other firms maintain a database of your clients, prospects, and schedule and will send pre-written e-mails based on a schedule you supply. For instance, you may want to send a series of four or five e-mails to each new prospect over the course of 60 days. These companies will ensure your e-mails are sent on schedule. For example, you might designate e-mail one to go out the day after you enter their data, e-mail two to arrive three days later, and e-mail three to be sent in one week. The company will make sure each prospect you enter receives the e-mails according to the schedule you provide. You write the e-mails, which are then "personalized" by the e-mail company by automatically filling in the prospect's name. These companies can save you time and ensure your communications stay on schedule, but they are not personal. This is still a one-size-fits-all format for your clients.

Whether you send postcards, newsletters, or e-mails, before you decide on a program, consider how important your communication program is to you, your prospects, and your clients.

Your Communication Is You

When you communicate with a prospect or client, whether the message is written or verbal, you're training the recipient to pay attention to you because you bring value to them—or you're training them to ignore you because you waste their time.

What does that mean to your program? It means every communication with a client or prospect is as important as your first. It means every time one of your prospects or clients hears from you, they are learning how valuable—or worthless—you are to them.

Every communication, no matter how small, says more to the recipient than the contents of the message. When you communicate with a client or a prospect, you are letting them know what you think their time is worth. You're also letting them know what your time is worth. Moreover, you're telling them whether you're different from the rest of the crowd--or just another salesperson with nothing to say and a lot of time to burn.

Communication with your prospects and clients—whether phone messages, email, or snail mail--*are you.* You may not be standing in front of them, but you're speaking directly to them. Would you take up that person's time with the same material if you were standing in the room with them? If not, then don't send the message.

What is Effective Communication?

Effective communication brings value to the client or prospect. Effective communication means never wasting a prospect's time. Effective communication means respecting your clients by giving them something that's valuable to them, not something that's valuable to you.

A typical salesperson gives little thought to communicating with their database of prospects and clients. The basic idea is to keep his name (and the company name) in front of the client. The assumption is the communication won't be read anyway, so just get your name in front of them to remind them you're still around.

We often think that anything we send is communicating, and as long as we're communicating, we're maintaining a relationship with our clients.

This type of thinking is just plain wrong.

One salesman has been trying to get my printing business for several months. In person, he's a likable guy. He's easy to get along with and personable. He's certainly persistent—I've told him no several times, but he still calls and sends me stuff. Will he ever win my business? No. Why? He's a time waster. He never has anything of value to share. When he calls, he wants to chat about anything and everything, but he never offers anything of value *to me*. He appears to have nothing better to do. I've learned to avoid his calls.

When he sends stuff, which is constantly, it goes straight to the trash. What does he send? Jokes, cartoons, odd news stories. Things he thinks are funny. And his quarterly newsletter? It doesn't contain anything of the slightest interest to me. There's little to nothing about printing, business, the economy, or anything else of importance. He sends more jokes, recipes, and household maintenance tips.

Nice enough guy. But he's wasting his time and resources pursing me. He has trained me to ignore him because he has no respect for my time. He may have nothing better to do than sit around finding jokes and cartoons, but I certainly have better things to do than read them. He may think he's building rapport. In fact, his communication has taught me to avoid him at all costs.

We all know people like the print salesperson above. They mean well, yet they drive people away.

Your communication with prospects and clients may be doing the same thing to you. How do you know whether your communication is working for you or against you? Just ask yourself a few questions:

- Would I want to hear from me?
- Do I bring something of value every time I communicate with my database?
- Do I know what the people in my database value?
- Do I have a distinct purpose for every communication, or do I communicate just to get my name in front of them?

- Do my communications show respect for my prospect or client's time?

- Are my communications designed to benefit the recipient or benefit me?

You may not like the answers if you've been honest with yourself. If you don't feel you can be objective, ask someone else to look at the items you send out and evaluate them for you.

Even if your communications add value, do they demonstrate your trustworthiness? Value is important, but your communications also reinforce—or undermine—the trust you have worked hard to build with each prospect and client.

When you commit to sending something, do you send exactly what you commit to sending, exactly when you say you will send it? Failing to follow through on communication commitments is just as big a sin as any other failure on your part. "But," you say, "I was really busy and couldn't get it out today like I promised. I'll get it in the mail tomorrow. Besides, the prospect won't even notice if the package doesn't get there until a day or two later than he expected." You may be right. However, what if you aren't? What message does that send to your prospect?

The Interior Decorator: In Houston, as in every other city in America, many professionals try to stay in touch with potential prospects and their clients by using newsletters.

In April, my wife and I received a newsletter from an interior decorator. Since this was the first newsletter we received from her, I assumed we had only recently been added to her mailing list. Debbie, my wife, may have met her or spoken to her, so she decided we were candidates and she put us into her system.

The mast of the newsletter carried a publish date of January/ February. We received it in April. This is not good. Nevertheless, I assumed that since we were new in her system, she was just catching us up to date with the newsletter. I assumed she was probably giving herself an opportunity to hit us with several communications in a short period of time.

The newsletter was fairly well done and with quality content to boot. I didn't think any more about it until August when we received another newsletter, this one dated as the May/June issue. Now, this was a real problem. The first issue had a reasonable excuse for coming so late—it was a catch up mailing. But, this one? She had no excuse to get the May/June issue out in August. Moreover, what happened to the March/ April issue? We didn't get one.

Would I consider using this decorator? Probably not. If this is how she handles her small commitments, how does she handle her major commitments? I have no intention of finding out.

Several salespeople who have heard this story think I'm being too hard on this woman. "After all, it's just a newletter," they say. "Who cares when or even if it goes out? Besides, how many people are going to notice it was late to begin with?"

I don't know how many other people noticed, but I did. Besides, this is more than a newsletter. It is a serious business commitment she has offered her prospects and clients and which she failed to meet. This is not a person I want to hire.

We all have commitments. We all have obligations we voluntarily accept. Those commitments are just as important as any other commitment we make—and they demonstrate our trustworthiness just as clearly.

Sometimes those commitments are inconvenient. Sometimes, they're a pain in the rear. That doesn't give us the right to ignore the commitment.

Like everyone else, I have commitments I must keep, whether I feel like it or not. My POWER SELLING newsletter is a twice monthly newsletter that goes out on the first and fifteenth of every month to the thousands of salespeople, managers, executives, professionals, trainers, coaches, and business owners who subscribe. Every issue has two feature articles—one written by a guest trainer and one written by me. Twice a month, on set dates, like it or not, I have to have the newsletter completed, edited, and queued to send. In over two years, I have never missed a deadline, nor will I as long as I am healthy. Would my readers notice if I missed the deadline by a day or two? Many wouldn't. Actually, probably most of them wouldn't. I'm not going to find out. My commitment is my commitment—it's a reflection of how good my word is. That means I'm sometimes up at 2 A.M. composing an article I don't really feel like writing. However, the deadline doesn't care whether I feel like writing or not. The deadline is the day I promised the newsletter would go out, and it makes no difference how I feel.

Not only do your client and prospect communications indicate how well you respect their time and your trustworthiness, your communications also provide insight into your professional competence, or incompetence, as the case may be.

Factual and statistical errors, exaggerations and overstatements all communicate lack of competence. Whether you're sending an article, a letter, or a report, make sure your information is accurate and up-to-date. Never assume your information is the only news your prospect or client is getting about your subject. Your object is to inform and educate, not confuse. If your information is inaccurate or outdated, why should a prospect or client have faith in anything else you say?

Using superlatives about yourself, your product, or your company can also damage your credibility and trustworthiness. How often have you received a letter, brochure, or flier that proclaims the author to be a great expert who raised himself from nothing to a millionaire in less than a year, and his product will change your life? And your response? You probably blew it off as total hype.

However, what if someone you knew and respected said the writer of the brochure was the greatest in the world? What if people you could actually talk to claimed the product changed their lives? You would probably take the claims much more seriously.

You can use superlatives. You can make strong claims about yourself, your product, and your company. You can make any claim you want as long as you have someone else who is fully identified, credible, and can be contacted—make the claim for you.

Testimonials are a time-honored part of marketing. The more recognizable and trusted the person making the claim about you or your product, the more believable the claim. That doesn't mean normal customers can't be effective messengers. In some cases, they can be more effective than well-known figures. However, if you use an average customer, you must fully identify that person's name and location. If the claim relates to a business purchase, include the person's company if possible. (This is not always possible as some companies have rules about their personnel identifying themselves as employees of the company in an advertisement or testimonial).

As worthless as a claim of superiority made by you or your company, is identifying a customer identified by only their initials, such as C.D. or their name with one initial, such as B. Thomas, or Thomas B. No one believes these testimonials any more.

Credibility and trustworthiness are hard to gain. Don't fritter it away with worthless claims and unverifiable endorsements.

Constructing an Effective Communication Program

The more personal you can make a communication, the more effective it will be. Yet, constructing a prospect/client communication program that's highly personal, focuses on the concerns of the people in your database, and touches each individual on a pre-set schedule can seem like an overwhelming task.

Yes, such a project takes time; but the benefits in added sales, increased referrals, and stronger word-of-mouth advertising can be enormous. Consistent, targeted, personal communication that shows your prospects and clients you value them and their time is one of the most lucrative projects you can undertake.

How often should you communicate? This, to some extent, depends upon your particular sales process. The type and number of communications you have with a prospect will vary according to your sales cycle, the demands and needs of the prospect, and the complexity of the sale.

However, our focus is on a maintenance communication program, not a sales communication program. Therefore, we'll concentrate on the mechanics of establishing a maintenance program only.

Depending on the marketing guru you read, you'll find people suggesting you develop a contact program with as few as 6 "touches" a year (a touch is any contact with a prospect or client—in person, phone, e-mail, postcard, letter, whatever), to as many as 33 touches a year.

How many touches are necessary? The general concensus tells us that 12 to 16 touches a year is both realistic and effective. Use less that twelve and you won't make an impact. Use more than sixteen and you may be accused of stalking.

With fourteen touches a year, you will have some communication with your client or prospect about every four weeks.

How do you make these fourteen touches? Different people respond to different media. One may respond to a letter, another to a phone call, another to e-mails. Since your program is going to be automated, but with as much personalization as you can manage, take these differences into account and design a program that touches them in several different ways.

Unfortunately, cost is sometimes an issue. For some of us, even a single letter mailing to the database can be too costly. A series of letters may be way out of reach.

However, for most salespeople, cost can be managed. The key is to mix the communication methods so each person in your database will get several communications during the course of the year that "speak their language."

For example, a fourteen-touch campaign might consist of:

- two formal letters (at about 53 cents per for a single page letter)
- two phone calls
- four post cards (at about 58 cents per bulk, or about $1.20 personalized through SendOut Cards)
- four e-mails
- one birthday card (at about $1.75 per card)
- one holiday card (at about $1.75 per card)

For someone with a database of 350 people, this campaign would only cost about $2,400 per year, assuming the salesperson is responsible for all costs. If the company pays postage, the cost is only $1,442 per year, or about $120 per month.

If even this small cost is too much, the birthday or holiday card can be replaced with an additional letter, reducing the cost by $427 per year, to an average of only $180 per month – even if you pay for postage.

Another possible combination would involve adding a quarterly newsletter:

- two formal letters at 53 cents per letter
- one personal phone call
- four quarterly newsletters via e-mail at $19.95 per month using an e-mail service such as www.aweber.com
- three post cards at 58 cents each
- three e-mails
- one birthday or holiday card at $1.75 each

This schedule reduces the cost, with postage, to $1,832 per year. For those lucky enough to have a company pay the postage, that's only $1,108 annually, or $92 per month. You would be hard pressed to develop a quality contact program that's highly personal and touches your entire database for less than this amount.

Yet, for most of us, the number and type of touches and the cost is the least of our worries. The real issue is: What do we communicate that has real value and how do we keep it from becoming a full-time job?

We'll begin by looking at content, since that's often the biggest problem. Content is king. As Seneca said at the beginning of this Key: it is the quality that counts, not the quantity. You want to train your prospects and clients to pay attention to you, not ignore you.

Let's step back and look at the typical things salespeople communicate to their prospects and clients.

First, there's the waste of time phone call—the "have ya made a decision yet?" call or the "I just wanted to check to see if there's anything I can do for ya" call. These calls are time wasters; an empty excuse to call the prospect to remind him the salesperson exists and wants his business. If the prospect had made a decision or needed something from the salesperson, he would have called.

I'm not saying you shouldn't pursue the prospect or make calls. Just don't waste the prospect's time. Empty calls add nothing of value for the prospect. In fact, they take value away by wasting her time. But with thought and preparation, you can convert these calls into a value added experiences. Instead of an excuse to remind the prospect you exist and want her business, the calls can be used to enhance your value to the prospect.

What do you have that can add value to your follow-up calls? Possibly, there have been significant changes to the product or service that enhance your ability to meet the prospect's needs. Maybe you know about something in the economy or industry that might alert the prospect to forthcoming changes that will affect her decision about your product or service. Possibly your prospect or her company recently made the news and you can congratulate her. Perhaps you add information that provides a deeper understanding of how your product, service, or solution will increase their bottom-line, making your proposal more cost effective. Whatever the justification for your call, you must bring something that makes your prospect's time spent on the phone with you worth the investment on her part.

Prospects, especially business prospects, do not accept calls or return calls when they don't see value in the time they'll be investing. Prospects don't have someone screen their calls because they want to be rude—they screen calls because salespeople have taught them that sales calls are time wasters. If you want your calls answered or returned, teach your prospect that spending a few minutes with you is time well spent.

Likewise, prospects have been taught by salespeople to ignore e-mails—again, they waste time. E-mails can be an even bigger time waster than phone calls. Not only do most emails not bring value to the prospect, many are barely readable. Here's a recent e-mail I received from a salesperson after we spoke on the phone:

Dear Mr. McCord,

Thank you for taking the time to speak with me morning. I hope your day is going well and that you have the opportunity to think about what we talked about earlier. I know your busy but I think we can help you with your tele-communication needs and reduce costs a whole lot.

Not only are we one of the largest tele-communication providers in the world, we have a ton of services that we will add to your bill every month.

If you have any questions, I am always available. I will call you early next week to see what you want to buy.

Sincerely,

Not only is this awkward to read, the garbled message indicates the salesperson's company will add on to my phone bill a "ton" of other services as well. Now, obviously, he meant to tell me his company can provide other services and add these to my bill should I choose to purchase, making payment and tracking of costs simpler (uh, has he ever seen a phone bill? I doubt having these services added to the phone bill will make tracking costs easier.). Because this e-mail was so sloppy, I had to spend time trying to translate it into English.

Instead of wasting my time with this e-mail, the salesperson could have given me additional information on why I would want to switch companies; he could have sent a cost comparison; he could have sent an article on how great the company's products are; he could have sent an article about the excess costs companies incur if they aren't watching their tele-communication costs. While we were on the phone, he heard my miniature daschund, Mr. B.J. barking in the background and I commented I was going to have to find out how to help Mr. B.J. learn not to bark. He could have attached an article about training your dog not to bark. That would have been a highly personal and relevant touch.

Letters, postcards, newsletters, and other communications from salespeople often suffer from the same maladies as the phone calls and e-mail above. There isn't a clearly defined purpose for many of these communications other than to get the salesperson's name in front of the prospect or client.

If you concentrate on delivering value to the people in your database instead of getting your sales message across, you will be more successful at both. Letters, newsletters, voice mail messages, e-mails, postcards and any other secondary communications with prospects and clients can inform and educate; they can reinforce; they can encourage the prospect or client to take an action; and they can help spark interest. They cannot sell.

Trying to turn these communication opportunities into miniature salespeople is a mistake that drives salespeople to concentrate on the sales message, not the value the message can bring to the recipient.

Your rule of thumb should be: If it doesn't add to the relationship in some way, it isn't sent or the call isn't made.

After you understand the consequences of wasting your client's time and learn what does add value, that still leaves the personalization issue. Creating communications that are personal and add value is a serious "how to" problem.

A number of techniques can increase the personalization of basically non-personal communications. Obviously, personalizing a phone call is not an issue—by nature, it is personal. Personalizing an individual letter, birthday card, or e-mail also is not an issue, since each is a unique creation designed for a single person.

However, do you really want to create a unique letter or e-mail for each communication with a group of prospects and clients?

Every salesperson has a basic set of letters and e-mails that must be sent to prospects and clients on a regular basis. These may range from updates on their purchase to requests for additional information from the prospect. Since letters and emails are common, you needn't bother recreating the content each time you have to send them. Nevertheless, they should be personal communications. The easiest method is to write a strong letter to use as a template. This letter will be the same for everyone who receives it, except for the first paragraph. Emails can be handled in the same manner.

Write the letter or e-mail and save it. When you need the letter, open it, fill in the appropriate name and address, write a custom first paragraph, then print and send. This simple template method of handling ordinary communications will save a tremendous amount of time over the course of the year. Instead of reinventing the wheel, you simply add one unique spoke. Instead of taking fifteen to twenty minutes to write and proof your letter, you spend five minutes customizing it for each recipient.

And your mass communications? They're more difficult, but still manageable with a little effort and creativity.

Bulk letters can be personalized through articles and other items you might include with the mailing. Of course, you will construct your address merge to insert each prospect or client's name in the greeting and possibly one or two places within the body of the letter. That still isn't personal enough. Adding an article you've selected for each recipient to the mailing will make each letter seem more personal.

While this may sound like a lot of work, it isn't that difficult or time consuming. As a test, I created a mailing for a small sampling of 350 subscribers to my newsletter and checked to see how long it would take me to create a personal mailing that was bulk in nature.

Each person received an identical letter except for the name, address, name in the greeting, and the person addressed by first name one other time in the letter—and the article I included with the letter.

I divided the mailing list into five groups: financial planners, real estate agents, mortgage loan officers, high tech salespeople, and a mixture of salespeople and professionals from a number of industries. For each of the first four groups I found an article that would interest them from a source most of them probably hadn't seen. The fifth group received a new report on the anticipated future growth of the U.S. economy.

I spent about 45 minutes to write and edit the letter. I spent another hour and a half finding and photocopying the articles. Merging and printing the letter and envelopes took about an hour. Stuffing the envelopes, including selecting the appropriate article, took another hour and a half. To create and mail the entire mailing took about four hours and forty-five minutes, or a bit less than one minute per letter mailed.

The same process without the articles took two and half hours. For the investment of an additional two hours, I turned a typical mass mailing into what appears to be a personal mailing, with an article selected for each individual recipient. In addition, for about twenty percent of the recipients, I wrote a personal note on the article.

Finally, I repeated the original process with my wife helping. I created another database of 350 of my newsletter subscribers and started over from scratch. The entire process took about three hours. For the investment of an additional half hour (and the help of my wife) instead of sending a standard bulk letter, I created a more personal mailing that added more value for the recipient.

This relatively small investment of three to four and a half hours, twice a year, isn't much. For an investment of less than the equivalent of one working day, you can personalize your letters to a much higher degree than most of your competition. A little extra work on your part creates a great payoff.

Bulk e-mails: You can create a similar process by using an e-mail service such as aweber.com. With Aweber, you create several e-mail databases and customize your e-mails in the same way you customize letters by attaching articles or other material.

I split my e-mail database into a group of 350, with five different groups within the larger group. This time, it took about 45 minutes to write five separate e-mails (one for each group to be e-mailed) and about 45 minutes to find appropriate articles. I then attached the articles to each group of mailings, scheduled the mailings and waited for them to be sent. The total process to design and send 350 semi-personalized e-mails took about an hour and a half—about fifteen seconds per e-mail.

Again, the process was reasonably quick and produced a mailing that appeared to be personal. In addition, as a side benefit I can use the same letter and e-mails again, saving the writing and editing time the second time around.

Newsletters: Aweber or a similar service is also an excellent choice for creating and distributing newsletters. Although the process takes more time and a great deal more work, you're probably better off writing your own newsletter rather than buying a canned one.

Canned newsletters save time and look professional, plus they contain articles by professional writers. That's where their advantages stop and their disadvantages kick in. First, they can be expensive, depending upon the service you use. The biggest issue you face is, heaven forbid, your prospect or client may get the exact same newsletter from one of your competitors. Now, how personal is that?

By using a service such as Aweber, you have the freedom to create your own newsletter, personalize it with each recipient's name and company, attach additional files, and include links and other options. Most companies have a selection of newsletter templates you can use.

Finding content is easy with the Internet, although at least some of the content should have your own byline. Other articles are available through Internet article sites such as Ezinearticles. com, articleworld.com, articlehorizon.com, articleson.com, myarticlepub.com, and hundreds of others. On the other hand, you might prefer to search out well-known authors who publish articles about your industry and ask if you can reprint one of their articles in your newsletter. Most will be happy to accommodate you as long as you give proper attribution.

By creating your own newsletter, you can control the content—meaning you not only control the articles, but can also insert company and product/service announcements, special promotions, and other overt advertisements. Including promotions and ads is perfectly acceptable as long as they remain a minor part of the newsletter.

Postcards: Postcards are more difficult to personalize because unlike letters, e-mail, and newsletters, you don't have control of the printing process. You will probably buy off the shelf postcards or have a company such as Quantum Mail custom print your design. Either way, every postcard is identical. However, that doesn't mean there's no solution. There is. It's a little time consuming, but worth the extra effort.

Rather than employing a company to print and mail your postcards, have the company print the cards and ship them to you. You'll address and post them. While you're doing that, use a high-quality pen and write a short personal note on each card.

Time consuming? A bit. Again, I tried this with a database of 350 people. To print address labels, post the card, and write a short note took about three hours. If I made four postcard mailings a year, I would have to invest about one and a half workdays—but that's over the course of a year. Not a great deal of time and effort for the payoff.

In another experiment, I took the same number of people, but this time I addressed each card by hand. My time investment? It doubled to six hours for 350 people, or a little over one minute per card. Is it worth doubling your time investment to address each card by hand? In my opinion, it is. I don't believe investing a minute per contact is unrealistic, and it eliminates the obvious bulk format of an address label.

Birthday/Holiday cards: By necessity, these must be personally addressed and the message must be hand written. A birthday or holiday card is supposed to be a personal greeting from you to your client, not a mass produced obligation you're fulfilling.

Every year I get two types of cards from businesspeople—those that are obviously bulk and those that have obviously been handled by a human.

I receive birthday and Christmas cards from people with whom I've done business for years, and the cards have an address label on the front and a machine printed signature. What does that mean? It means they didn't send me a card. Rather, it means I'm in their database—period. The card is nothing more than their fulfillment of what they believe is a marketing obligation.

On the other hand, I receive a few cards that have obviously been addressed by a human, signed by a human, and a human wrote a short message specifically to me. Those cards I truly appreciate. The sender cared enough about me—or their image—to give me the impression the card is personal. I always assume it is—even though I have no idea who actually addressed it, signed it, or wrote the note. For all I know, the sender had an assistant do all the work. Still, I appreciate the gesture—and I certainly remember who took the time and consideration to send it.

Copywriting and Editing: Salespeople are seldom good copywriters and editors. Copywriting and editing are arts that take practice, skill, and creativity. Consequently, just sitting down and jotting something is not going to cut it. Like anything else in high-level sales, you need professional help.

Hiring a professional copywriter or editor for your most important pieces is a great option. Unfortunately, good copywriters don't come cheap. Good editing isn't cheap either.

An alternative is to obtain basic education in copywriting and editing. You'll probably never become a professional, but, then, that isn't your goal. Your goal is to prepare well-written copy that's clear, free of grammatical and spelling errors, and will influence your readers.

You can also find competent copywriting and editing services through colleges and universities, where graduate students and faculty members moonlight for extra money. This is usually cheaper than hiring a professional, although the competence level of many of these people is on a lower level than the professional. Still, they'll probably do a better job than you could accomplish on your own.

On the Internet you can find copywriting help from Dr. Joe Vitale at www.mrfire.com, Shel Horowitz at www.frugalmarketing.com, The Marketing Sherpa at www.marketingsherpa.com, and at Copywriting Information Center www.copywriting-information.com.

Creating and implementing a multi-touch, highly personal communication campaign need not be expensive or onerously time consuming. With a small financial investment and a reasonably small time investment, you can create a program that touches each prospect and client multiple times a year, using several different media. All it takes is a little planning and the commitment to personalize the program as much as you can.

Unless you have a massive database, your total investment for the year will only be a few hundred dollars per month and your time investment will add up to only a few days or weeks per year. Your return will be worth far more than this small investment.

> **Design and Schedule Your Communication Campaign**
> Determine your communications for the next 12 months and put the schedule on your calendar. Decide the communication mix, basic topics, and the delivery schedule. Once you've created the basic schedule, go on to design and write your first five communications. You'll find it's easier to write several at once when you "get in the groove." Once you have several completed, you're more likely to maintain your schedule. After you deliver your fourth communication, design and write the next five.

Summary

You should now have:

- A complete year of prospect and client communications planned out, including

  ❖ The mix of communication media you will use

  ❖ The basic topic for each communication

  ❖ The date each communication will be sent

- The first five communications should be fully designed and written, with the exception of any articles that will be included with the communication

- You should know what your communication campaign will cost and have the expense budgeted

Now that you have your campaign scheduled and a little over a third of it designed and written, be aware that things may change. If an event occurs that allows you change your campaign, don't hesitate to do so. Remember, nothing in your marketing plan is etched in stone. Everything is flexible. Reacting to fluctuations in the economy, the industry, or society is the fun part of marketing.

Marketing must be dynamic, not static. Your goal is to help shape the way your prospects and clients think. To do that, you must become aware of outside factors that influence their thinking. You have an opportunity to proactively shape their thinking as you take advantage of outside forces.

Approach your communication campaign as a fun challenge, not as drudgery. Creating a campaign that helps your prospect and client see the value you bring, sets you apart from the competition, and reinforces your reputation and integrity can be incredibly satisfying.

This is an opportunity to use your creativity and discover hidden talents. Have fun! Above all, remember—you can do this. You can create a great campaign. You can learn and apply a few basic skills that will turn your communications into great ambassadors for you.

More importantly, if you want to become a superstar, do what the superstars do—add value to everything. Teach your prospects and clients to pay attention because you, unlike your competition, value and respect their time.

Additional Resources

You'll find examples of client letters and emails, as well as links to additional communication resources such as copywriters and editors at www.thetwelvekeys.com,/html/communication.html.

Key 9: Developing the Skills You Need— Finding the Right Training

Natural abilities are like natural plants; they need pruning by study.
— **Sir Francis Bacon**

*M*any non-salespeople view the sales profession as something to do when you can't do anything else. They think salespeople lack marketable skills or technical education. Not only is selling viewed as a last resort for those who can't get a "real" job, people assume that in order to be successful, you must have a special knack – the gift of gab combined with the ability to persuade people out of their money.

Even some salespeople view their profession in this unflattering light. They don't believe someone can learn how to sell, nor do they believe they can become better salespeople. Either you have the knack for sales, or you don't. Nothing you can do about it.

If this were true, not many salespeople would actually make a living.

While researching my book, *Creating a Million Dollar a Year Sales Income: Sales Success Through Client Referrals*, I spoke with four dozen salesmen and women across the United States and Canada, each of whom earn more than a million dollars a year. In terms of income, these folks are the cream of the selling profession. Each of them brings in more money per year than most salespeople earn in a decade—more than some will make in their lifetime. Yet, of these four dozen superstars, only three considered themselves "natural born" salespeople. Forty-five people told me they possessed raw natural talent in people skills, marketing savvy, or the ability to work through rejection and keep going. Nevertheless, this natural talent got them nowhere until they learned to improve those talents and learned other skills. Doing so required a considerable amount of their free time and income as they pursued learning opportunities beyond the training their companies provided.

Although they've reached the top of their professions in terms of income, these men and women still invest enormous amounts of time and money in personal training. On average, they spend between six thousand and eight thousand dollars a year on training—not including what they spend for a personal sales coach. Despite their great success, they spend at least five hundred dollars a month on books, CD's and DVD's, seminars and conferences, sitting in on tele-conferences and webinars, and other forms of training.

Of course, with their high incomes, eight thousand dollars a year isn't that much. However, look at what these superstars do on average during the course of a year:

- Buy and read 23 sales and business books, and numerous periodicals, white papers, and articles

- Spend about one hour per day reading

- Buy and absorb 25 sales and business CD's or DVD's

- Spend an average of almost 1.5 hours per day listening to CD's while traveling

- Attend two conventions or conferences per year, attending four seminars or workshops per event

- Attend four additional seminars, tele-seminars, or webinars a year

- Attend an additional two seminars or workshops per year put on by their local or state associations

  Let's put those numbers into real terms:

- They spend 240 hours per year reading sales and business books and materials

- They spend 360 hours per year listening to training and motivational CD's or watching DVD's

- They spend 14 hours a year attending seminars and workshops

That totals 614 hours per year, or just over fifteen 40-hour work weeks a year spent on personal training—and this doesn't include the time each person spends with a personal sales coach.

If these superstars need that much training, what do the rest of us need?

Many salespeople are confused about training. I'm often asked, "How do I know what kind of training I need, and how do I decide which events to attend or books to buy?" With thousands of sales books, CD's, DVD's, seminars, tele-seminars, white papers, articles, and other material readily available, the choices can be mind boggling.

In this Key, we'll look at these questions and develop general guidelines to help you decide what major skills you need to learn and where to get the training you need.

As with the other subjects we deal with, these are guidelines to help you find your way, there are no absolute answers since each is at a different place and all have different needs.

How Do You Find a Quality Trainer?

Selecting a sales trainer or a sales training company isn't easy, because you have thousands of choices that include well-known trainers or companies such as Brian Tracy, Jeffrey Gitomer, Tom Hopkins, Huthwaite, Sandler Sales, and so forth, as well as individuals and companies you had not heard of until you ran across their products.

Your best training choices may not come from the household names. Your best choice may be a trainer about whom you know little or nothing. With so many choices and so many lesser-known names, how can you make a rational choice about where to spend your training money?

Unfortunately, to some extent you won't know the answer until you've paid your money and read the book, listened to the CD, or completed the training. However, you can do several things to help make a rational decision before you invest.

What is their specialty? Before you spend money, determine the trainer's area of specialty. If she specializes in sales techniques and you need prospecting training, you probably want to look elsewhere. Few sales trainers have the skills and ability to be experts in every phase of selling. Most specialize in one or more areas, although their training may cover other areas in which they are not specialists. Unfortunately, if you choose an area outside their specialty, they probably won't tell you you're about to take training in a subject that isn't their specialty.

Finding a trainer's specialty requires a bit of detective work. As you examine their products and promotional materials, you may notice they emphasize one or two areas more than others. It's a safe bet they specialize in those areas and are most comfortable working there.

Some trainers declare their specialties up front and only work within them. I recommend you look for a trainer who knows his or her expertise and works exclusively within those areas.

Read their articles. Most established trainers have written articles that should be available on their websites. Read several articles to get a feel for the trainer's style, message, and content. As you read, ask yourself:

- Does this person have anything new to contribute or is this just a rehash of common knowledge?

- Does he give real world examples or just speaks in general, theoretical terms?

- Does what she says make sense?

- Is this information I can actually use?

Be aware that reading only one or two articles can give you the wrong impression of a trainer. You may have accidentally picked one or two of their best or worst articles, giving a false impression. To be fair to both you and the trainer, you need to peruse a broad spectrum of his writing. Not every article a trainer writes will be of value to you, no matter how good the material. And not ever article a trainer writes will be topnotch. And to consider spending money with them, you should find at least one or two articles that address your areas of concern. If not, then look elsewhere.

In addition to reading their articles, look to see which publications have published the trainer's work. National and association business and industry publications such as *Sales and Marketing Management, Selling Power, Advisor Today, Realtor, Senior*

Market Advisor, Registered Rep, and other national publications are selective in what they publish. If the trainer has material published in a few of these publications, she's probably delivering something of value.

Has he written a book? If he has written a book, check to see if it was published by a traditional business book publisher such as McGraw-Hill, John Wiley and Sons, Warner Press, Career Press, Morgan James Publishing, Kaplan Press, or another major publisher. Major publishing firms only accept about 3% of the submissions they receive. This doesn't mean they don't occasionally publish junk—they do. Yet, their selection process is so rigorous that the chances are good a trainer published by one of these large firms has a lot to offer.

What if a trainer's book is self-published? Non-traditional publishing through self-publishing and vanity presses is so common that over half the sales books on the market are now published through non-traditional methods.

Many fine books are being self-published, along with a lot of junk. The problem with self-publishing is that anyone can do it and there's little quality control. Anything can be self-published. Many people who don't write well or don't have a message strong enough for a traditional publisher resort to self-publishing. Being self-published doesn't mean a trainer's work isn't worthy of being on the market, but it does mean you can't use the publisher to help qualify the quality of his training.

Before you sign up for a training seminar, I suggest you read the trainer's book, which should highlight his best, most innovative thinking and reflect his specialty areas. If you don't want to invest in a book, borrow it from the library or skim through it at the bookstore.

The website. Analyzing a trainer's website can give you a great deal of information about the quality of the training she provides. Like any other company, sales trainers and training companies must sell their products and services. They're selling expertise and the ability to train others in that expertise. Declaring you're an expert isn't good enough. You have to demonstrate.

Most quality trainers provide added value on their websites. Look critically at the site's contents. If all you find is a sales pitch, you should probably move on to another trainer. If you find quality articles and tools offered without charge, this trainer has earned your serious consideration.

As with published articles, the site's content should give you an understanding of where their expertise lies.

Endorsements. Check the endorsements a trainer receives from other trainers and business leaders. Do people you know and respect endorse this person? If so, you have some basis for your decision, although endorsements should never be the deciding factor.

Claims: As with any communication campaign we discussed in Key 8, be wary of self-pronounced superlatives or unrealistic claims by the trainer. Are there things you suspect he can't deliver? Does he promise you'll be an overnight success without having to work? Quality trainers want to help you improve your skills, but they won't promise to work miracles. In sales, there are no miracle cures—only skills that must be learned that will help you move from the bottom to the top of the pack. However, these skills are not secrets known only to a select few who charge enormous amounts of money to enlighten you. Easy, fast, miracle cures don't exist, although many trainers claim otherwise. They appeal to your greed and feed their own greed.

Pricing: When you purchase a CD or DVD, register for a seminar or tele-seminar, or pay for any other training, you aren't paying for the cost of the CD or even for the trainer's time. You are paying for the trainer's knowledge, expertise, and the content of the training. And if the trainer has developed a big enough name and reputation, you're paying a premium for that.

Although not all one-hour CD's are of equal value, the market has set a price range between $15 and $90—usually $25 to $50. Is a CD by Brian Tracy at $79.95 three times as valuable as one for $24.95 by a lesser-known trainer? The answer to that question is a personal decision based on your needs—and on the quality of the training offered by the lesser-known trainer. Both CD's fall within the accepted price range dictated by the market. But what about the one-hour CD for $695.00 by a trainer you've never heard of whose website is nothing but an infomercial? The quicker you can click away from that website, the safer your money.

Judging a trainer by his pricing is reasonable, but that should never the deciding factor. You need training, and quality training is going to cost money. Quality trainers are just that—quality trainers. They are not hucksters looking for a one-time kill. They are not rip-off artists looking for the sucker. They aren't promising a miracle cure that for only $895.00 will turn you into a top producer overnight.

Applying the above criterea to trainers who ask you to spend money on their programs will help you make rational decisions about investing your training dollars. This selection process isn't foolproof and you may still find you've invested in a book, CD, or seminar that didn't provide what you hoped for. Still, by eliminating the hucksters and concentrating your money on quality trainers, you will make your training investment go further and help your business grow.

What Training Do You Need?

Besides finding the best trainer for your needs, you also need to decide what type of training will help you at each stage of your sales career. Dozens of areas within the sales and marketing process require specific skills. Few of us have the natural ability to perform well in each area. A typical salesperson must be proficient in:

- Lead generation and prospecting
- Communication—both oral and written
- Listening
- Questioning
- Presentation
- Persuasion
- Basic public relations
- Recognizing and overcoming objections
- Closing
- Negotiating
- Customer Service
- Interpersonal Relations
- Basic marketing

• Internet marketing

Most of the skills you need fall into one of the above categories. At first glance, you might wonder about some of the areas I listed. Why does a salesperson need public relations or Internet marketing skills? Because most salespeople don't effectively use public relations and because the Internet will play an ever-expanding role in your prospects' decision-making. One is an opportunity missed by most salespeople; the other is gaining in importance. Skill in both areas is a must-have for salespeople who want to stay competitive in today's marketplace.

Planning Your Training Agenda

Your biggest challenge is getting started on a self-training program. Once you fall into the habit of studying, you begin to miss your training time if you skip a few days. Like all of selling, training takes time and dedication. However, unlike most aspects of your career, your training is something you can have absolute control over. You decide what to study, from whom, and when.

Another issue with training is finding the right time, but this should be your easiest decision. How much time do you spend in your car? Time spent driving can be prime training time.

Do you have a set time every morning or evening when you review the day's activities and plan for the next day? If not, you should. Increasing that time by only thirty minutes a day for reading and study will do wonders for your training.

If you spend an hour a day in your car listening to training and motivational CD's or audio books and thirty minutes a day reading, you'll invest 360 hours in training during a typical year.

That's equal to forty-five full days of training—or the equivalent of about eight college courses. How many of your competitors are improving themselves at that rate? I'll bet few, if any.

With careful planning you can work in a couple of seminars or tele-seminars and possibly even a state or regional convention or conference. If you've established your set training time, adding seminars, conferences and association meetings will only add a few hours per month, if that much.

Discipline and focus are the keys: Discipline to establish and maintain your training schedule, and focus to determine and follow your course of study. It isn't necessary to set out a full year's training when you establish your calendar, but you should at least have a broad idea of your plans. Set your training schedule in sandstone, if not granite.

We can't take any credit for our talents.
It's how we use them that counts.
Madeleine L'Engle

 ### Schedule Your Training Time

Decide how much time you're willing to commit and set a schedule you can maintain for self-study and improvement. Go back to the calendar you've created and enter your self-study time for each day of the year. Look at the commitments you've already made and establish a daily time for self-improvement, preferably at the same time every day. You'll find it's easier to maintain a habit if the time is consistent.

Determine your course of study for at least three months at a time. Most people can read an average-size book in six to twelve hours. If you read for thirty minutes a day, five days a week, you'll spend about thirty hours a quarter reading. You should be able to read at least four books per quarter, sixteen a year.

The typical CD is an hour long. If you listen to each CD five times, you can hear twelve a quarter, based upon an hour's listening per day. You'll absorb forty-eight CD's a year.

Sixteen books and 48 CD's a year. A year from now, if you read the books and listen to the CD's and apply what you learn, your business should be well beyond where you are today. If you buy each book and CD, you'll be investing $1,500 to $2,000 dollars in your sales library. However, a library card can cut that in half, because most of the books and audio resources you need are available in your local library. If they aren't, talk to your company about establishing a company library. If they won't, consider exchanging books and CD's with other salespeople in your company. Money should never be an excuse for not getting the training you need.

In addition to books and CD's, you will find hundreds of articles on each of your subject areas at web sites such as www.salespractice.com, www.salesopedia.com, www.eyesonsales. com, www.salesgravy.com, and www.bestmanagementarticles.com.

A particularly fine source of training can be found at the Top Sales Experts site--www.topsalesexperts.com. Top Sales Experts is a group of a couple of dozen handpicked trainers. This group of top trainers covers almost every aspect of the sales process, from prospecting to customer service and everything in between. Each trainer has been vetted and selected because of their quality.

Select At Least Your First Three Areas of Self-Study

From the areas above, select the first three topics you plan to study. Though you may choose to spend many hours on a particular subject, set out a logical progression with at least three areas so you know where you'll go after you finish each subject. Decide if you'll start by honing your best skills or focusing on a weaker area. I suggest you schedule your training to begin with areas that will immediately boost your sales pipeline and your income, and then work toward the area that will have the least immediate impact. Getting quick results will encourage you to continue your self-study program.

Schedule each topic into your calendar, giving each topic one to two months. Schedule two months for complicated topics or ideas you want to study in depth. If you find you haven't scheduled enough time, adjust your calendar as you go along. This is not a race; it's your business. Give yourself the time you need to understand and implement what you learn. Consistency is crucial, but how long it takes to work through a particular area is not.

Summary

At this point, your completed calendar should include a marketing schedule, communication campaign, and your self-study program.

Since your calendar probably contains only a portion of your commitments for the upcoming twelve months, you'll have to make time during the year to update and finish your planning. At the beginning of the last month in each quarter, schedule time to plan the next quarter. Waiting until you have reached the end of scheduled events will tempt you to "take a little break." Little breaks have a way of becoming big breaks. Big breaks will kill your momentum.

So far, you've done a tremendous amount of work. You have:

- Reconstructed your sales history

- Discovered your strengths and weaknesses

- Determined exactly what time and money you're willing to invest in your business both time and money

- Researched and determined your marketing channels

- Researched and determined your marketing methods

- Made sales and income projections based upon your marketing plan

- Scheduled your database communication program and designed some of the communications

- Determined and scheduled your self-training program

Congratulations! You've completed more work than 90% of the other people in your industry. You are one of a select few salespeople who know where you're are going and how you'll get there. Besides that, your new plan is realistic and workable, not based on guesswork or a farfetched hope. You've created a roadmap for the future based on solid research, historical reality, and your personal commitment. This plan is your pathway to success.

Perhaps you're wondering: How will I turn this into reality? You've committed to a life-changing program, one that challenges you to stretch beyond your comfort zone. If you're feeling doubt and anxiety about how you will get there, don't fret. Our next topic will show you how to make your plan a reality.

Additional Resources

At www.thetwelvekeys.com/html/training.html you'll find an extensive discussion of various training areas, along with recommended books and websites as great starting places for your self-study. These books and sites provide an excellent introduction to each area, but are only a starting point, not the only resources you should study. Each area is huge and reading a couple of books won't give you the background and useful information you need. However, those resources will get you started on the right track.

In addition, I address a number of prospecting, training, and personal marketing issues each month on my blog, http://businessresearchdatabase.com/SalesandManagementBlog/, which has been nominated as best sales and management blog.

Key 10: Turning Plans into Reality — Turning Giant Steps into Small Steps

*The man who removes a mountain begins
by carrying away small stones.*
— **William Faulkner**

To this point, you have done a lot of analysis and a good deal of planning. Now, you're faced with implementing all of this and making it work.

This may all seem like a monumental challenge. Overwhelming even.

Superstars have learned a great secret about their business that is so obvious—but so easily overlooked by everyone else. They don't have to do it all at once. They don't sit around on January 1st of each year thinking, "My, gosh, how in the world am I going to make a million dollars this year?"

Their focus isn't on the result; their focus is on what they have to do *now* in order to guarantee they'll have made the million 365 days from now. They concern themselves with what they must do now to make their objective a reality.

Your concern is the same. You don't have to become a superstar overnight. It's not one giant leap, it's one step at a time. If you carry away enough small stones, you'll move the mountain—exactly the same way the superstars do.

Learning to stretch to reach goals and objectives that seem out of reach involves cutting your goals and objectives into smaller, more manageable pieces. Rather than looking at your income projections for the coming year and thinking, "how in the world am I going to double my income in just twelve months," chop that goal into small segments.

Your goal isn't to double your income all at once, but increase it over a period of 52 much smaller segments—actually, over 365 tiny segments of only 24 hours each. Instead of having one giant mountain to move, you have 365 small stones to move, each small stone getting you closer to your ultimate objective.

It's not the load that breaks you down, it's the way you carry it.
— **Lena Horne**

Most of the work you have done to this point has been creating the broad outline of your plan. You've planned where you want to go, and in broad outline, how you're going to get there. You have been looking at how to become a superstar from the macro-planning mode.

Now, it's time to think in a micro-planning mode, turning that mountain of work into 365 little stones that combined make up the mountain.

Looking at the big picture is daunting. Looking at just what you need to accomplish on a daily and weekly basis is not such a hurdle to overcome. If one of your objectives is to make 3,000 cold call dials per month, that's only 150 per day, or if you plan to call for 5 hours during the day, 30 dials per hour, one every two minutes. Since most of the numbers you dial will probably not be answered or will be answered by voice mail, you will probably be on the phone less than 20 seconds on 80 or 85% of your calls. That's 24 calls an hour that you are on the phone less than 20 seconds each, or about 8 minutes during the hour. Of the six calls where you reach someone, most will be short calls, probably less than 3 minutes. One may be as long as 5 minutes. That is a total of about 28 minutes out of every hour actually on the phone. You can do that. That's not that intimidating.

If your goal is to set five appointments a week from your cold calls, that's only one per day. Again, that's not intimidating. That is only one appointment out of every 30 phone calls where you talk to someone. You can do that. In addition, if you manage to set your one appointment early in the day, you're now working on tomorrow's calls. You're already ahead of the game.

The key is to break your objectives down to manageable bits—bits that you can accomplish, not giant objectives that seem out of reach. In effect, to date all you have done is define the outcome you desire, not the detailed little actions and goals that will get you there.

Certainly, your sales and income objectives have been stated as definitive goals. "I'm going to make $150,000 this coming year." You have also stated objectives within your marketing methods. "I'm going to make 3,000 cold calls per month." Now, you set your mini-plans in place to reach those objectives.

First, Get Organized

Organizing your time and space can help you reach each small goal.

Take a day or two to get yourself organized before starting on your new programs. Make sure you have all of the basic "stuff" you will need. If you plan on a cold calling campaign, get your call lists together so you don't have to constantly stop and find new names and phone numbers. Make sure your list is free of any Do Not Call names and numbers. Make sure you have your script ready to go. Moreover, make sure you have a form to help you track your dials, your contacts, and your appointments.

If you intend to network through associations or organizations, decide now which organizations or associations and schedule any upcoming events. Don't wait until the last minute as it then becomes too easy to decide to skip. Get the association's schedule now, rather than later. If you have to RSVP or register for the event, do so now, while it's on your mind.

Spending time to get organized eliminates many of the excuses that can later hinder or even destroy your motivation. Procrastination is more likely to kill your goals than anything else is.

In addition to taking a day or two to get your workspace organized and to get the items you will need in place, plan on setting aside about 30 to 45 minutes each evening prior to leaving for the day to plan and organize the next day's work.

Get your call list in order, have your presentation materials ready to go, clear your desk of unnecessary junk so you have a clean start in the morning, and make sure any other supplies you will need the next day are at hand.

For most of us, getting started is the most difficult part of the day. We find excuses, we find busy work, and we visit with others in the office, and just generally waste time. However, most of all, we avoid rejection. Since prospecting is the primary function most salespeople engage in, rejection is an everyday experience. We hear "no" far more often than we hear "yes." Eventually, even for motivated salespeople, the rejection begins to wear us down. We begin to find creative ways not to be rejected and those usually involve procrastination.

Learning how to handle rejection is paramount to becoming a sales superstar because no matter what level you rise to in sales, you are still going to experience the "no's." Maybe not as often, but they will still be there. Moreover, for most of us, rejection is personal even though we understand intellectually that the prospect is rejecting our offer, not us personally.

Depending on how you market, dealing with a "no" can be a direct, in-your-face rejection, or can be an anonymous trashing of our direct mail letter. However, almost all of us must, at some point in the selling process, deal with face-to-face—or at least ear-to-ear rejection.

If you cold call, your rejection is immediate—and it can appear to be very personal. When you call a complete stranger and they hang up on you or rudely tell you to get lost, the tendency is to take that as personal rejection. The salesperson that has sent out a thousand direct mail letters suffers the same rejection; but is protected by not knowing the recipient didn't even look at it, but instead threw it into the trash. In actuality, the rejection is the same—the individual is rejecting your offer, not you. However, one salesperson hears in a loud, clear click his rejection, while the other never hears the soft slip of the letter into the trash.

Worse, once you get the opportunity to get in front of a prospect, the "no's" continue to come. You make your presentation.

You get your "no." You answer the prospect's objections—and you get your "no." You drive home your close—and you get your "no." Repeatedly, at times, it seems that "no" is the only word people know.

Then, finally, you get a qualified "yes." The prospect agrees to purchase if you can do a little something out of the ordinary. YES! Finally, someone who has his checkbook out and is ready to go. All you need is a little help from your sales manager. Then, it happens again. "NO." Sometimes you feel that you not only have to fight prospects, but your sales manager as well.

You managed to get your manager on board? Great. Now all you have to do is get the warehouse to agree to nudge a delivery in a little earlier than the calendar allows. Again, "no."

Do the "no's" ever stop? No.

Of course, there are the "yes's"—and that's what keeps you going, striving to get to the occasional "yes." However, all of those "no's" can stop you dead in your tracks if you allow them.

How you handle the "no's" is the key to how you get to the "yes's."

Attitude is one of the great limiters of salespeople. People have a tendency to anticipate outcomes and many times that anticipation has an influence on the actual outcome. If you approach a task with a defeatist attitude, there is a good chance that you will fail. If you approach the same task with an attitude of success, there is a good chance you will succeed. Why? Several reasons, but two are of importance to our discussion.

Success is often achieved by those who
don't know that failure is inevitable.
— **Coco Chanel**

First, if you assume you are going to fail, you need not give your best effort. Why should you? You already know the outcome before you even try to tackle the problem. After all, you know you're just wasting our time.

Secondly, your prospect can read your defeatism in your voice and body language. If you don't believe in what you're saying, how in the world can you expect a prospect to believe it?

Consequently, in order to be successful, you must be able to take the rejection you experience and deal with it in a positive manner. You have to find a way to eliminate the residual negative feelings you have from the rejection that seems to be all around you.

Advice for handling rejection has generally centered on either understanding that each "no" gets you closer to "yes," or understanding that, since the prospect doesn't know you as an individual, the rejection cannot be personal but is rather a rejection of the offer you made.

Both of these are true statements. For many, neither gives much solace.

So, if the traditional methods of dealing with rejection don't seem to work very well, what can you do to rearrange your attitude? You need to find a format that will give you the opportunity to offset the rejection with success. You need to institute a program that will allow your brain to regroup and experience the joy and positive reinforcement of getting the "yes's" that offset the "no's."

How can you create a method to give your brain the positive "yes's" it needs to readjust after receiving a chorus of "no's"?

One method that many find successful is to set aside tasks during the day where you know you will experience success. You have a contract to sign with a new client? Try to schedule it later in the day, after you have done your cold calling tour of duty for the day. End the day on the positive note of signing a contract. Have a couple of very strong referrals to call? Again, make the positive calls after you have made your cold calls. Save the best for last.

Some salespeople have found that reversing this schedule leads to more productive prospecting. Having just come from signing a contract or having made two very successful calls to strong referrals gives them the positive mental attitude needed to sound strong and convincing on the phone when they make their cold calls.

Better yet, try to arrange your schedule where you have two or more positive tasks to perform each day and split them up so your brain is readjusted several times during the course of the day. The more regularly you can feed your brain positive experiences, the easier it is to deal with rejection. Rejection becomes the exception, rather than the norm.

Creating Bite Sized Goals

You will achieve a grand dream, a day at a time, so set goals
for each day. Not long and difficult projects, but chores
that will take you, step by step, toward your rainbow.
— **Og Mandino**

Taking your big objectives and turning them into bite size goals is not difficult.

In order to establish goals, whether monthly, weekly or daily, they must meet seven criteria:

Simple: The goal must be simple. A goal of making 200 cold calls in a day or making four sales this week. Each is a simple goal. Straightforward. Easy to understand. Easy to track. Easy to know whether you have reached your goal or not.

Being simple doesn't necessarily mean being easy or that getting there is not difficult. It simply means that the goal itself is not complicated.

Specific: The goal must be specific. In the two examples above, the goals were both simple and specific. If the goal is not specific, you don't know whether you have reached your goal or not. A goal such as colding call for 5 hours is not specific because you can waste a tremendous amount of time in 5 hours. Just because you were at your desk for 5 hours doesn't mean you were actually performing the task. The goal of cold calling for 5 hours is nothing more than a time objective, not a cold calling goal.

Objective: The goal must be objective, meaning measurable. If you cannot measure it, it isn't a goal. The two goals above are simple, specific, and measurable. Either you made your 200 cold calls or you didn't. Either you made you four sales for the week or you didn't.

Reasonable: The goal must be reasonable, meaning it can be achieved. In the cold calling example above, what is a cold call? Do you define a cold call as a dial or as a contact? It can be defined either way with corresponding measurements. If your definition is dials, then 200 a day is a reasonable number. If you define cold calling as contacts, then 200, although specific, is not reasonable.

Written: Goals must be in concrete, not in vapor. Write each of your goals, even a daily goal, down. Putting something in writing makes it more real, more concrete. Once written, it becomes your goal, until then, it is nothing but a wish.

Public: Although not a "rule" in order to have a goal, broadcasting it to someone--a co-worker, mentor, coach, spouse, or sales manager--also makes the goal more real and concrete. You now have someone besides yourself to verify and monitor your accomplishment. Making the goal public, even to just one other person, obligates you to reach your goal.

Believable: The goal must fit within your belief system. If your personal belief system refuses to accept the goal in either terms of your ability to reach the goal or your system of ethics, you don't have a goal. In Key 12, we will discuss your belief system, but anything that goes against your belief system becomes difficult or even impossible to do.

Again, this doesn't mean that it cannot be difficult. It doesn't mean that you cannot question whether you can actually reach the goal. It means that if your belief system completely rejects the idea of reaching the goal, it becomes impossible to reach. On the other hand, if your ethical system rejects the actions you intend to take—or the intended outcome—the goal should never have been a goal in the first place.

Each evening, write out your specific, objective, reasonable, simple goals for the next day. Allow your mind to contemplate your next day's goals during the evening and while you sleep. Allow yourself to become comfortable with the next day's challenges so when you arrive at the office the next morning, you are alert and ready to tackle the day's work.

Furthermore, keep your days uncluttered. Your goals list for any single day must be manageable. If you create a dozen goals for a day when you know you simply don't have time to reach them all, all you will accomplish is frustrating yourself and creating guilt.

Reaching your goals today gives you energy and strength to help you reach tomorrow's goals. Setting yourself up for failure will simply sap you of your strength and your enthusiasm. Allow your day's activities and goals to stretch you, but don't allow them to stretch you to the breaking point. Goals are to be met and conquered; they are not intended to conquer you. Goals are meant to take you one small step closer to your big objective, not to set you back.

Your daily goals are not your minor "need to do" items. Your daily goals are those things that take you one small step toward your primary objectives. All of us have things we need to do, but those things are not goals. Sending that thank you note is important and you need to do it, but it isn't a goal. Returning the call to your most important client needs to be done, but it also isn't a goal.

In addition, we are talking here only about your professional goals, not your personal goals. Certainly, those other goals are important. In fact, many of those goals may be far more important than your business goals. However, the goals you set for yourself during your business hours are business goals.

When conflicts arise between your goals and your "need to do" list, choices must be made. Evaluating which is more important is sometimes fuzzy. Nevertheless, keep your priorities in order. Which is more important, making the cold calls or attending the networking meeting, or checking on an order for your client? Both are important. One you must perform yourself, the other may well be better performed by someone else—someone in customer service or shipping. If you choose to do the legwork yourself to run down the information for your client, you're allowing your goals to be trumped by busy work that is simply taking up your production time.

Indeed, busy work is your worst enemy. We all must engage in busy work to some extent. Life is full of busy work. Still, you cannot let busy work divert you from your real goals. You must free yourself of busy work or schedule it after you have met your true goals.

Finding ways around the "need to do" items and the daily distractions isn't always easy, but it is always necessary.

Don't answer the telephone. For most salespeople, answering the phone is second nature. We do it without thinking. Yet, the phone is one of our biggest time wasters. Simply discipline yourself not to answer it during the hours that you have set aside to accomplish your goals. Rather, put a voice message on your phone informing clients, prospects and others of the two specific times during the day you will return calls—and stick to it. If you are in a position where you may have actual emergency calls, acquire a second cell phone and only give the number to those who might actually have an emergency and let them know it is for real emergencies only.

Don't hang around with the other salespeople in the office. Gossip, the never ending moaning and groaning by low producers about how bad things are, and the discussions of last night's game are career killers. Your time is valuable. In fact, your time is the only thing you have to sell. Let the low producers give their time away by wasting it; you invest your time in your future. Hanging around low producers not only wastes time, they may contaminate you with their attitudes and work habits. The only thing low producers can teach you is how to fail.

Don't bring up the Internet unless you must in order to get a particular task completed. Once that single task has been completed, log-off. The Internet has become a tremendous time waster. I know. I am a news junkie. If I could, I'd be checking news sites every five or ten minutes—and then spending twenty minutes reading the latest news stories, which means I have to go through the sites again immediately to see if anything new happened while I was reading the "latest" news. And guess what? Ninety nine percent of those stories don't affect me in the least right this second. I'll find out about them in due time. My solution is to keep the Internet shut down unless I actually need it. I simply remove the temptation to "just take a quick look to see what has happened."

Take your dreams, your big objectives, and chop them into little bites. Then focus on those little goals. Next thing you know, those big objectives are not so big and unmanageable anymore.

Set Daily, Weekly and Monthly Goals

Set out your small, manageable goals for each day and week for your first month. Make your objectives reachable. Focus only on goals that will help you reach the major objectives of sales, income, marketing and training that you have established in your marketing plan. Everything else is a "need to do," not a goal. Then find ways to eliminate the need to do's.

Summary

You should have your workspace organized. You should know exactly where you are going and, now, how you are going to get there—one small step at a time. The objectives you have set out in your business plan are reachable. They don't have to overwhelm you. They're just 365 little steps all put together in one large objective. Concentrate on the 365 little steps and let the big steps take care of themselves.

Additional Resources

At www.thetwelvekeys.com/html/goals.html you'll find a number of articles and resources regarding setting and meeting goals.

Key 11: Accountability—
Finding Your Coach or Mentor

Accountability breeds Response-ability.
— **Stephen R. Covey**

*E*ach of the previous ten Keys has presented challenges and tasks with the promise of immense potential rewards if Keys 1 through 10 are taken seriously and implemented fully. The rewards come only after hard work and probably more of an investment of time, energy, sweat, and money than you had anticipated when you originally picked up this book. As stated in the introduction, this book is about the unspectacular preparation for spectacular results.

The unspectacular preparation you are currently doing is the same preparation the superstars do. They may not do it in the same manner that you are doing it now, but they go through each step you're going through. Moreover, they have support from others, just as you need support.

You need not, should not—and cannot—do it alone. Certainly, a few souls will be able to take this book and implement these Keys without needing someone to help them over the discouragements, the problems, the failures, and the disappointments that will come. They are the exception, not the rule. Furthermore, there is no need to go it alone. Trying to reach the top as a lone wolf is not only unnecessary, it greatly increases the likelihood of failure.

Implementing these Keys, no matter how well you have researched, how well you have planned, and how well you execute will not be without failures and setbacks. They are part of life and they will happen. Furthermore, there will be days when you just don't feel like doing what you need to do in order to be successful. Additionally, you'll face unanticipated roadblocks that seem to appear at the least opportune time.

Everyone, no matter how successful, faces these. You cannot escape them.

Consequently, you need someone who can help you face and address them. You need someone who is sincerely interested in you and your success who can give guidance, support, and a swift kick if necessary. You need a supporter, a cheerleader, a guide, and even an enforcer. In short, you need someone who will praise you in your successes and hold you accountable for your failures. Like the CEO of a company, which you are, you need a Board of Directors to oversee your progress, help identify problems, and reinforce those things you do well.

Spouses, friends, relatives, and sales managers can play this role. Almost anyone can play some role. Certainly, it's possible to have multiple individuals involved, each playing a different role in your success.

However, in order to be as effective as possible, you need someone who has been where you have been, knows what you are going through, and has no stake in your success, other than a desire to see you succeed.

This typically eliminates your spouse, your friends and relatives, and your sales manager. Each has some stake in your success, whether income for your spouse or sales manager, family pride for a relative, or maybe even a negative interest such as jealousy or envy from a friend. Having a vested interest in you can lead to unwanted consequences such as impaired judgment, resulting in decisions based more on hope than reality.

What is the solution? Finding a mentor and/or coach, paid or not, to help you realize your full potential. A mentor and a coach are different. Generally, the mentor is an older, more experienced salesperson from within the same industry as you. The relationship can be formal or informal. Most often mentors are local and don't receive financial gain from the relationship. Coaches, on the other hand, are most often paid and I believe should be experts in their fields, but not necessarily in your industry.

Is there value in working with a mentor or coach? Almost all top managers and salespeople have had one or more mentors during their career and a large percentage either have had or currently have a coach.

When conducting interviews with the 47 million dollar a year income mega-producers for *Creating a Million Dollar a Year Sales Income: Sales Success through Client Referrals*, I discussed mentoring and coaching with each. Over 80% of these superstars have had one or more mentors during their career; and over 75% have had at least one sales coach during their career. Moreover, over 30% of these men and women who are at the very top of their industries, making huge annual incomes, still have a mentor and over 65% still have a sales coach that they work with.

Mentors and coaches can be vital to your success. If the most successful people in the business need mentoring and coaching, how much more those who have not reached that level of success?

Still, a mentor or a coach is only one part of the growth process. Mentors and coaches don't replace the self-training discussed earlier. Rather, they supplement and compliment your self-training program.

Mentors

What a mentor is: A mentor is usually defined as a trusted guide, a counselor to a younger, less experienced person. Although there are now paid mentors, the original concept entailed a relationship where the mentor had no financial interest in the relationship, but rather performed as a mentor simply due to either a belief in the future of the mentee or as a form of giving back to the profession.

Most mentor relationships are informal, where a younger salesperson seeks out a respected older salesperson for guidance and counseling. These relationships can last for only a short time or go on for long, extended periods.

Mentors typically give advice and counsel based on the needs and questions of the mentee. In these informal relationships, seldom is there a rigorous, systematic approach to the mentee's business.

In addition to the advice and guidance given by the mentor, they are often the role model for the younger salesperson. Their personal success and growth inspire, teach, and help direct the mentee by example.

How to find a mentor: The temptation may be to look at the most successful salespeople or managers in your company or local leaders within your industry as potential mentors. These men and women may certainly be great mentors, but they may not be the best mentor for you.

Selecting someone to approach as a potential mentor involves more than simply his or her position within the industry or company. You have certain areas that you want to improve. You have areas where you need guidance and accountability. Your mentor should be strong in the areas about which you are most concerned. If you are looking for a mentor to help you work through the sales process, the best managers may not be your best choice. If you are looking to develop management skills hoping to move into management, the top salesperson may not be your best choice, either. Likewise, if your goal is to become a strong referral salesperson, selecting a mentor who is weak in referral selling but strong in another prospecting area would not help you develop the business you are seeking to build.

When looking for a mentor, you have several options. SCORE (Service Core of Retired Executives) offers free mentoring services at local offices throughout the country, as well as e-mail mentoring for those who don't have access to a local SCORE office. SCORE mentors come from all industries, and most functions within those industries. Finding one with the specific industry background you want near you may not be possible.

As mentioned, there are a number of individuals and companies offering fee-based mentoring. Again, finding someone with the specific background you desire may be difficult, and the concept of fee-based mentoring is contrary to the traditional mentoring model. Moreover, as with anything else you pay for, you will find excellent fee-based mentors and complete charlatans.

There are self-appointed mentor organizations who "certify" mentors and then promote their mentoring services through the organization. Are these certifications worth anything? Probably not, although it is an indication the certificate holder has been through some type of mentor training.

Unless you are in a highly specialized position, you should have no problem finding a quality mentor without having to pay for one.

Your local industry association or chamber of commerce may have a mentoring program, many do, usually without a fee. These programs often offer the opportunity to acquire a top-notch mentor within a more formal, detailed mentoring program with formal structure, guidelines, and a specific set of skills that the mentor must meet. A mentor found through these organizations will probably have participated in mentoring training.

If your local association or chamber hasn't developed a mentoring program, look for individuals within your industry that have the experience, skills, and business model you want for yourself and approach them with your request to enter into a mentoring relationship. Seldom will you be turned down.

In addition to finding someone who has the experience and skills you seek, make sure you get a mentor who can and will assume the role you wish them to play. Are you looking for the cheerleader who will pick you up, pat you on the back, and assure you that "you'll get 'em next time?" Alternatively, are you looking for a mentor that will hold you accountable for your actions in a more aggressive, straightforward manner?

Having to have the "perfect" mentor is a fallacy that stymies many from moving forward in acquiring a mentor. There isn't a perfect mentoring match and if you wait to find it, you'll lose out. You probably don't want Mr. Whipple or Nurse Ratchet as your mentor, but if those are your only options, maybe it's time to move. Find a quality role model who has the skills and experience you seek to develop and that you can reasonably work with—and approach them to take you on as a mentee. Better to have a good mentor that exists than a perfect mentor that doesn't.

Your responsibilities: As the mentee, you will have the responsibility of managing the relationship. Your mentor is giving their time and expertise to help you advance your career. They are investing themselves in you without any return other than their own personal satisfaction. Expecting them to manage the relationship simply is not realistic in most mentoring relationships.

Just as you must be the one to seek out your mentor and originate the relationship, you must be the one who sets up each meeting and keeps the relationship going. Your mentor is busy and freely giving you the benefit of his or her wisdom. Honor their time and their schedule by taking the burden of your mentoring off them as much as possible. Certainly, you work around their schedule; they don't work around yours.

Besides managing the relationship, you have two additional responsibilities:

- Taking advice and counsel. If you have done your homework and selected your mentor well, you should have no hesitation accepting their advice, guidance and counsel. If your nature is to resist constructive criticism and guidance, you will have to find a way to accept it from your mentor. They are there to help and their counsel, and criticism when it comes, is to help, not hurt.

- Taking initiative and implementing the counsel. Simply taking advice and counsel is, of course, not enough. You must implement. If you fail to implement the counsel you have received, you've wasted your time and more importantly, your mentor's time.

A mentor cannot only help you develop the skills you need and give you solid guidance based on their experience of doing exactly what you are seeking to do, they can help to hold you accountable for meeting your goals. Your mentor can be your "board of directors," the one to whom you must report your activities, your successes and your failures. Your mentor holds your feet to the fire—chastising you when you have failed to live up to your commitments and obligations, and praising you when you overcome the obstacles and potholes you will find in your path.

Working with a mentor: Once you have found your mentor there are a few housekeeping duties you and your mentor need to perform.

Prior to beginning the mentoring relationship, anticipate and work out some basic, agreed upon procedures. Discuss openly how you will handle disagreements, schedule conflicts, email correspondence and phone calls between meetings, and other areas that might become issues. Make sure you and your mentor are on the same page.

Besides the basic housekeeping discussion, make sure your mentor is in agreement with your mentoring goals and objectives. Let them know upfront what you hope to gain from the relationship and what you are looking for them to contribute. Don't expect your mentor to monitor your goals if you haven't asked them to do so. Of course, if you have chosen Nurse Ratchet as your mentor, you won't have to ask; she'll do it and make you pay dearly if you don't fulfill them.

It is only fair that your mentor be given full disclosure at the beginning of the relationship as to what you expect. Likewise, your mentor should give you full disclosure of both what they are willing to do and what they expect of you.

Sales Coaching

Coaching is usually a very different animal than mentoring. Coaches usually are paid on a contract basis and are individuals who may or may not have an expertise in sales or the particular area you are seeking coaching in. Some coaches specialize in a particular segment of the sales process; others claim to coach all areas of sales; others claim to coach all areas of sales and marketing; and some even claim to be sales, business, life, love and any other kind of coach you want them to be.

As with mentoring, there are certification programs for coaches and like mentoring, they are probably worthless. There are no universal coaching standards. All coaching certifications are by self-appointed authorities, usually with a coaching system or "coaching the coach" program to sell.

Coaching types: There are almost as many coaching types as there are coaches. However, by observation, the general rule tends to be the more fleeting the coaches' background in sales, the more "touchy feely," "self-discovery" the coaching tends to be. The more solid the coaches' sales background, the more direct, overt guidance and teaching the coaching tends to be.

One coaching theory holds that a coach only ask questions and let the salesperson discover the answer within him or herself, what I'll refer to as the "Metaphysical" theory. The Metaphysical theory believes that salespeople will be better served and make changes more rapidly if they discover answers on their own rather than being taught. The salesperson is questioned by the coach and is then left to contemplate the answer. Eventually through astute questioning by the coach and the salesperson's grappling with the questions, the salesperson becomes enlightened and once enlightened will implement their newfound knowledge.

The "Dictator" theory takes a much more draconian view of coaching. Here the coach is the expert teacher and taskmaster, the cracker of the whip. Obviously, this is the other extreme from the first theory.

Most coaches are somewhere in the middle of these two extremes. Coaches have their own view of what their responsibilities in the coaching relationship are and their own philosophy of coaching. Consequently, selecting a coach is not easy.

What a coach cannot do: Before we actually discuss how a coach can help, we need to eliminate any false hopes of what a coach might be able to accomplish. A coach can do great things for you and your business, but a coach cannot:

- Motivate you. Only you can motivate yourself. A coach can give a short spurt of motivation, but like any outside motivation you receive, that motivation is short-lived.

- A coach cannot force you to succeed. A coach can encourage, prod, and even give a quick kick, but no one can force you do something, you must do it:

- A coach cannot do your work for you.

- A coach cannot give you the desire or the commitment to succeed. Like motivation, you, not an outside force, internally generate these.

- A coach cannot make you like your job. If you hate what you are doing, find another job, a coach isn't going to help.

- A coach cannot make you perform.

- A coach cannot save your job for you. If you are close to being let go for underperformance, a coach may not be your best choice. Coaching is not an overnight cure all.

If the above are your hopes when contracting with a coach, you will be very disappointed. Neither a coach nor anyone else can do those things for you. Only you can do them.

What a coach can do: However, a good coach can help you do a great deal. The operative word in the last sentence is *help*. We have already established the fact that a coach cannot do anything for you; you must do it. Nevertheless, a coach can help you accomplish great things:

- A coach can help you develop the tools and skills needed to succeed

- A coach can help you analyze your sales history, your strengths, your weaknesses, and your vision

- A coach can help you develop your business and marketing plan

- A coach can help you implement and work your plan

- A coach can give discipline

- A coach can give encouragement

- A coach can give insight and wisdom from years of experience
- A coach can give in-depth, personalized training
- A coach can give a broader, more objective view of your market
- A coach can be a sounding board
- A coach can help you grow your business more rapidly
- A coach can help you plan and work toward your career moves and advancements
- On occasion, a coach can run interference for you

The above is a sizable list of benefits for a relatively small investment in your career. Not every coach can do all of the above. If you choose a sales coach that is not highly experienced in sales, many of the above potential benefits will not be available to you. Additionally, if you choose a coach you cannot get along with, virtually none of the benefits listed above will be available to you.

Selecting a coach: A coach can have an immense impact on your career—both positive and negative--in a relatively short time. Your selection of a coach must be handled with care. Don't allow yourself to visit a coaches' website and make an emotional decision to hire the coach based on the coaches' message on their site. Take your time.

Prior to making any decision about whom to hire, do some research via the Internet. You will find a variety of processes on the Internet for finding information on sales coaches. You'll find individual experts such as myself and many of the other experts referenced in the training section of www. thetwelvekeys.com; you'll find coaching groups and companies;

you'll find coaching organizations and associations; and you'll find coaching referral services.

Each has advantages and disadvantages.

Individual sales experts give you the advantage of working with a known expert in the areas you want to work on. These men and women have the knowledge, background and expertise you are seeking. Make sure that you will be working with the actual expert as some bring you in based on their name and then have you work with a coach they have hired. If you are not going to work with the expert, find out whom you would work with and why the expert is not the coach. Although most expert coaches are reasonably priced, some charge enormous fees, even if you don't work with the expert himself or herself but with a hired coach.

Coaching groups are usually companies offering many different types of coaching, not just sales coaching, and they usually have a number of coaches on staff or retainer. Groups can provide coaching quickly whereas your preferred expert may or may not have an opening at the time you wish to start a coaching relationship. When contemplating a coaching group, vet the coach assigned to you to determine if they really have the background and knowledge you want in a coach. Depending upon the coaching group, you may be given an opportunity to select a coach from their staff or they may simply assign one to you. Prices through coaching groups can range anywhere from very cheap to just as expensive as the most expensive expert.

Coaching associations and organizations are often groups that "certify" coaches and the coaches they set you up with are individuals that have paid their fee to go through the organization's coaching program. As with coaching groups, a good deal of care must be taken and you must thoroughly investigate the coach. Again, as with coaching groups, you may be given the opportunity to select your coach or you may have one assigned. Coaching prices typically range from relatively inexpensive to average or slightly above average.

Referral services typically act as matchmakers, taking your objectives and goals and seeking to match you with an appropriate coach. Most often, you will be referred to several, probably three whom the referral service believes meet your needs, from which you select the coach you want to work with. Referral services may save you the time of researching coaches, but, then, the coaches they refer may not be to your liking. If they don't meet your approval, the referral service will give you more names. Ultimately, this process may not save you much, if any, time. The coach you hire through a referral services pays the referral service the fee.

No matter the process you decide to use to find a coach, take the time to interview a number of coaches prior to entering into a contract. A good, quality coach will be happy to spend 30 minutes to an hour with you without charge to determine if they are the right coach for you. If you are dealing with a reputable coach, during the interview process, they should be evaluating you, just as you are evaluating them. A quality coach won't accept you as a client if they don't believe they can be of real service to you. On the other hand, some less responsible coaches will accept anyone's money.

During your interview with your potential coach, ask yourself:

- Do they have the experience and expertise in the areas about which I am most concerned?

- Is this person listening to me or simply giving me a canned presentation?

- Can I work with this person for an extended period?

- Is this a person from whom I can take objective criticism?

- Is this person a leader or follower? That is, do they take charge of the conversation or simply follow your lead. Whichever, that will probably be their coaching method.

- Does this person know about what they are talking?

The above are the questions you are asking yourself during the conversation. There are specific questions you want to ask the coach:

- I am most concerned about areas X, Y, and Z. What is your experience and skills in those areas?

- What specifically is your coaching philosophy?

- How often and for how long will we be speaking directly?

- What do I do if I need you between calls?

- What is your coaching procedure?

- Are you the person I will be working with all of the time?

- If not, whom will I be working with and can I have the same introduction process as this with him or her? If the answer is no, then ask "why not"?

- Why should I hire you?

How many coaches you interview depends upon you. I would certainly suggest you interview a minimum of three, more if you have not found someone with which you connect. Three interviews should give you a feel for various coaches. If you have researched well, you should be able to find your coach without having to interview dozens of individual coaches. Nevertheless, even if you believe your coach is the first you interview, keep interviewing potential coaches until you are comfortable you know the coach that can meet your needs the best and that you can work with effectively.

As with mentors, don't expect to find the "ideal" coach. They don't exist. No one is going to be everything you want in a coach. If you decide to interview until you have found that perfect coach, you will be interviewing forever. Just as with a mentor, a good coach you can work with is much superior to an ideal coach you cannot find.

Coaching costs: Coaching is not an inexpensive investment in your career. Yet, price is not an indicator of the value of a particular coach and decisions should not be based on price. Some of the most expensive coaches are the least effective, while there are great coaches on the lower end of the pricing scale.

Most coaches work through contracts. A coaching contract may be as short as a month, others as long as two years. The typical contracts are for three, six, or twelve months. Each extension of time will have a corresponding reduction in monthly cost. Most coaches also have an hourly fee structure for those who want to hire on an as needed basis.

It has been reported that the average sales coaches' contract fee on a three-month contract is $187 per hour. This is misleading since it is an average, taking into consideration the least expensive new rookie coach with no experience in sales or coaching (but, hay, they have that "certification" that says they know what they're doing), to the most expensive coach. When you consider that this per hour spread is somewhere in the area of $25 on the low side to $5,000 on the high side, the $187 per hour is skewed.

Experienced coaching will typically run between $300 and $800 per month for four 45 minute or one-hour sessions. Again, there is no correlation between value and cost. There are great coaches in the $300 to $500 dollar per month range and complete charlatans in the $700 to $1,000 per month range. On average, expect to pay somewhere between $1,200 and $2,400 for a three month coaching contract. Some coaches will allow you to pay monthly, with a slight discount if you pay the quarterly contract upfront; others require the full investment at the time you sign your coaching contract. Longer contracts of six or twelve months will probably have a built-in discount for the extended commitment.

Jeff's coaching experience: Jeff, a coaching client of mine, has been selling financial services products for one of the largest insurance and financial services companies in the world for a little more than three years. His first two and a half years had seen a good deal of triumph and disappointment. Actually, it had seen far more disappointments than triumphs.

He didn't have issues with dedication and commitment. He worked long, hard hours. He didn't have an issue with desire. He wanted to succeed as badly as anyone did. He didn't have an issue with his ability to learn. He is a very sharp guy and a very quick learner and spent a great deal of time studying product, from the basic products to sophisticated applications to solve estate and financial issues. He also didn't have issues interacting with others. Jeff is quite likable, friendly, and is easy to get to know.

Yet, he was stuck in the middle of the pack in his company's production. Jeff was as average as average can get. If his company wanted to create the model of their average salesperson, all they needed to do was interview Jeff because he was it.

When I met him, Jeff was seeking coaching but he was not sure what he wanted a coach to help him do other than to improve his performance. He certainly knew something was amiss, he just couldn't figure out what was missing.

During our discussion, it became obvious that Jeff didn't have a plan; he hadn't spent much time learning to sell-- although he had spent a great deal of time learning his technical expertise, he had neglected learning how to generate the clients to use it with. In addition, he had a serious image problem with being an "insurance agent."

We established these were the areas that needed to be addressed immediately. From there we established a detailed plan, begin working on learning how to generate clients, and, the most important, changing his image of what he does for a living.

Jeff took the guidance and training I gave him and ran with it. He pushed me to push him faster. He tried everything we discussed and modified his selling process as he learned.

Nevertheless, more than anything, he began to see himself as an advisor to his clients, giving high quality advice and guidance, not simply selling products. His view of himself and consequently his profession changed. It certainly didn't change overnight and not without some resistance to using the term "insurance" in his title. Nevertheless, he has come to grips with what he does. He is proud that he can give his clients, their family and their business a solid financial footing from which to make their long-term decisions.

Jeff and I have been working together for a little over a year. During that time he has developed and worked through one marketing plan and is now on his second. He has developed and worked through one training plan and is now working on advanced marketing and selling methodologies. Most importantly, Jeff views himself as a strong, valued counselor to his clients, proud of who he is and what he helps his clients accomplish.

He's no longer the average salesperson in his company. He hasn't reached the top of the heap yet, but he is now in the top 25% of his company's producers. He almost doubled his income during the past year from where he was when he and I started. He's not satisfied with his current position in the company or his income. His goal this year is to reach the top 10% of producers in the company, again almost doubling his income. In addition, based on his commitment and dedication and his willingness to learn and implement what he is learning, he stands an excellent chance of reaching that goal.

When he and I began working together, he thought earning more than $100,000 in a year was just a dream. Having accomplished that, he firmly believes reaching the $200,000 mark is within reach. I sincerely hope he reaches his goal. I know he can. Nevertheless, as with all of selling, only he can do it.

Find Your Mentor or Coach

Knowing the value of having a mentor or coach, or both, should motivate you to take the initiative and seek out a personal mentor or coach for yourself. Do it now, while you are still motivated. If you wait, more than likely, you will find excuse after excuse why you will do it later and never get it done. Your career is too important to allow apathy and procrastination to side track you.

Summary

You should be in the process of finding your personal mentor and/or coach if you haven't already done so. You should know exactly what you are looking for in a mentor or coach—that is, what qualities and skills your mentor or coach needs. If money is a serious issue, look towards a mentor. Mentors will not have the time to invest in your career that a coach will and more than likely will not take the initiative in helping you direct and manage your career, but they can offer tremendous learning opportunities and give solid advice that you cannot get from family, friends, or even your sales manager.

If you can squeeze out the money, a coach can literally change your career. Hire one the second you can afford the sacrifice. Don't wait until you can easily afford one—hire one now, or as soon as possible. The quicker you hire a good coach you can work with, the sooner you will realize the benefits.

Don't look at hiring a coach as an expense; it is an investment. And realize that a coach will more than likely pay for him or herself quickly. If their fee is $700 per month and they quickly increase your sales income by $1,000, they have certainly justified your investment.

Additional Resources

At www.thetwelvekeys.com/html/coaching.html you can find a detailed discussion of my coaching philosophy. Read it and then use the questions it raises as you interview a number of other coaches.

You'll also find a number of articles on both mentoring and sales coaching to give you more in-depth information for your search for a mentor and coach.

Key 12: The Sales SuperStar Mindset

*We won't even attempt what we do not believe
at a deep level we can have or deserve.*
— **Ruth Ross**

$\mathcal{T}$o this point, we have spent our time discussing actions from researching your history to setting your goals to finding a mentor or coach. However, actions must be rooted in a foundation; otherwise, they lack power and effectiveness. Action without a solid foundation is wasted energy. There is no other profession besides sales where so much time, money, and energy is wasted on fruitless action.

The activities salespeople, managers, professionals, and companies engage in are not intended to be fruitless, of course. However, much of what they do is simply going through the motions, never expecting the results they wish for to come to fruition. In fact, *many fully expect their actions to fail.*

Yet, the superstar fully expects every action they take and every plan they make will come to pass. They're shocked if it doesn't.

Why would someone spend their time, money, and energy performing actions they expect will fail? Well, on occasion, these actions are well thought-out experiments, sales and marketing tests to analyze the effectiveness of a new method, product, system, or process. More often, they are performed because the salesperson or professional has been taught that the action is what you do.

There is no belief in the effectiveness of the activity performed. Even more basic, *there is little or no faith in the ability of the person performing the action to achieve the desired result.*

Our exploration of the Keys to success must shift from actions to the foundational structure of those actions, the mindset of the sales superstar. For if you lack the foundation necessary to effectively implement actions, you assure yourself of failure.

We've all seen the highly gifted football player who has immense God given skills. He's the player who is among the fastest, the quickest, the most graceful, and the strongest. His destiny is obvious. He cannot help but be one of the greatest running backs the NFL has ever seen. Who can catch him? If they catch him, who can stop him?

He earns a huge signing bonus; gets tremendous publicity; a city pins their hopes on him.

Yet, despite the hype, the anticipation, the talent, he proves himself an utter, total failure. He can't hold onto the ball. He whines and cries with every minor ache and pain, missing games for small injuries that frustrate and anger his teammates. He complains about the lack of support that his blockers give him. He's out of the league within only three or four years.

We're also familiar with his opposite. The low round draft pick from a small college that enters training camp making the league minimum. He, unlike the gazelle above, is slow. He lacks size, quickness and strength. Everyone wonders why he even showed up for camp, knowing that he will be among the first cut.

Notwithstanding their unquestioned knowledge of his future, he becomes a star. He always seems to find a tiny hole to run through. When hit, he seems to be able to bounce with the hit and keep going for a few more yards. His legs just seem to continue forcing him forward. Injuries? No one would know if he had any for he never complains. He simply does his job better than anyone else.

How can one with all the tools and gifts fail so miserably while another with no talent and no hope succeed so magnificently? Every year this scenario plays itself out in every sport and every sport's league across the world—and in every sales organization as well. The record books are overflowing with the impossible accomplishments of those that didn't have a chance of making a team, much less becoming a star. On the other hand, the unemployment lines are overflowing with those who could not possibly be anything but stars.

We run across men and women from each of these two groups so often that our vocabulary has words to describe them. Those who posses gifts the rest envy but who fail to exercise them we call underachievers; while those poor souls that God chose to deny any natural gifts but who excel way beyond what any rational person would believe possible we call overachievers.

Why do the gifted fail and the non-gifted succeed?

In a sense, the answer is easy. The "future superstar" flop lacks three key ingredients the "never should have been in training camp to begin with" star has: desire, commitment, and belief. Those three characteristics separate the superstar from the never made it. They're the characteristics of those who never had a chance but who by personal drive and force become stars despite the obstacles that kill the will of the average and also ran.

Desire: The Encarta Dictionary defines "desire" as "to want something very strongly, a craving." What is a craving? Again, the same dictionary defines craving as "a thirst" for, "a passion" for, or "a hunger" for something.

Desire creates the power.
— **Raymond Holligsworth**

The first thing that separates the man or woman who has the natural gifts but fails from the man or woman who may be without any real talent but finds a way to succeed, is a craving for success. The former may seek glory, fame, and fortune, but they lack the hunger to succeed. They want the accoutrements of success, but they don't crave being successful.

The one without talent craves success in their chosen field with all their heart. The accompanying fame and fortune is simply a by-product of their success. They crave excellence, not the by-products of excellence.

This certainly isn't to say that the overachiever doesn't glory in their success and fully enjoy the fame and fortune it brings. They most certainly do. However, the fame and fortune is not the motivating factor. Above all, they have a desire to be the best at what they do. They want to be, they must be, the best. They're unwilling to settle for less. It burns in their breast; it's their motivation, the ever-present voice encouraging them on to achieve.

Can desire be created? I've never seen it. I've seen motivational speakers create a small fire in a heart that burns for only a little while and then is extinguished by the reality of hard work. I have seen men and women who earnestly desire the *rewards* of success, but who have no passion to succeed. I have seen early success with accompanying rewards that didn't last because the success was not built on desire for success but desire for glory; and once the glory came, the work ceased.

Do you have a passion, a burning desire for success? If you do, you have the beginnings of a foundation to take you where you want to go. If you don't, find another career.

Commitment: Desire unfortunately, isn't enough. Desire without commitment is simply a wish. The Encarta Dictionary defines commitment as "steadfastness," "staunchness," and "dedication."

Desire gives you a burning hunger for success, but without the commitment, the steadfastness to endure the trials, disappointments, and necessary sacrifice, your desire becomes only a daydream.

Desire is the key to motivation, but it's the determination and commitment to an unrelenting pursuit of your goal—a commitment to excellence—that will enable you to attain the success you seek.
— **Mario Andretti**

"An unrelenting pursuit." Are you unrelenting? How many setbacks and failures are you willing to accept to reach your goal? How much pain and disappointment can you or are you willing to endure? How long are you willing to work ceaselessly to reach your objective?

Commitment doesn't guarantee quick results. John Barnum was a journeyman golfer on the PGA tour. He toiled at his golf game for years, never winning. He might have a decent tournament one week and then miss the cut for the next several tournaments. Nevertheless, finally, at age 51—a true dinosaur in golf terms, he won his first tournament. He was supposed to have been washed up years earlier. Yet, he persisted and finally, years after anyone else would have given up hope of winning, especially never having won on the tour before, Barnum did the impossible. He persisted because he had a passion to win, and beyond the passion, he had the steadfastness to plow through the years of disappointment and failure. Unfortunately, today Barnum isn't remembered for his unwavering commitment to success or for being the oldest first time winner on the PGA tour, but rather as being the first professional golfer to win a tournament using a PING golf club.

Or, take Daniel "Rudy" Ruettiger. If you haven't seen the movie "Rudy," do so. It is the quintessential move of desire, commitment and dedication to success. Still, like Barnum above, Rudy's success didn't come quickly, nor was it what he had envisioned. Rudy's success lasted one play from scrimmage. Too small to play for even a junior college football team, Ruettiger's dream was to play for Norte Dame, a football powerhouse, playing against the elite of college programs. The small don't play for Norte Dame or any other big name school. Nevertheless, Ruettiger would not take no for an answer. He toiled on the practice squad for four years, never once getting the opportunity to even suit up for a game. He was simply meat on the practice field for the "real" players to practice against and tear apart. And his reward for four years of being a blocking dummy? One game. One play. Yet, that one play fulfilled his dream. After years on the practice squad, he was allowed to suit up for his final home game. He saw action once--the last play of the game and the preceding kickoff. His reward for his years of sacrifice of blood and sweat was less than eight seconds—and a place in Notre Dame history as the only player ever carried off Notre Dame's field on the shoulders of teammates.

We need not stick with sports examples. Frank Bettger relates his experiences of failure and success in his book *How I Raised Myself from Failure to Success in Sales* (Fireside, 1992). Bettger relates how his life changed in two careers—professional baseball and sales through desire and commitment. His book is actually a sales training book, yet he relates the change in his fortunes in a frank, open manner. Furthermore, his discussion of his journey from failure to success is not related in terms of desire and commitment, those come out between the lines. Yet, unmistakably, they are there. As an aside, Bettger wrote another good book that is no longer in print, but if you happen to find a used copy buy it: *How I Learned the Secrets of Success in Selling*.

If you lack the commitment to succeed, just as if you lack the desire, it's time to find a new career. Few careers offer the emotional and spiritual abuse selling offers. This is not to say that you cannot survive in sales without the desire and commitment necessary to succeed, it simply is to say that you cannot excel, you cannot become a superstar without them. There are millions of average salespeople who simply survive, who simply manage to get through the day, who manage to make enough of a living to continue selling. That isn't success; that is mere survival.

Can commitment be developed? Possibly. You can force yourself to perform for a period, but eventually, if you lack the desire, your forced commitment will fade. Yet, if you have real desire can you force commitment? Yes, if you believe in yourself and your purpose. Commitment is not an either/or as desire is, but it emanates from your belief system about who you are and what you are capable of accomplishing. You can force commitment for a while and if the necessary desire and belief are there, that commitment will continue to grow until it becomes a natural part of your soul.

Belief: Failure is rooted more in a lack of belief in oneself and one's ability than in a lack of desire and commitment combined. Those who lack either commitment or desire cannot succeed, but the number of salespeople who are lacking in either pale in comparison with the number who just don't believe they can succeed.

In order to succeed, we must first believe we can.
— **Michael Korda**

Let's look as well at the definition of the word belief: "confidence in the *truth* or *existence* of something *not* immediately susceptible to rigorous proof." Synonyms are "conviction" and "certainty." The definition of conviction is "an unshakable belief in something without need for proof or evidence."

Your most deeply held beliefs are used by your mind to direct and correct your actions. You must eventually act according to your deepest held convictions about who you are and what you can do.

This doesn't mean that you cannot act outside of your belief system, for you certainly can. Everyone acts against his or her belief system on occasion—and probably more than just on occasion. Nevertheless, over time, we must submit to what we believe or risk some mental breakdown.

In essence, we are what we believe we are; we do what we believe we can do; we are who we believe we are.

Success follows belief, as does failure. Maybe not swiftly. Maybe not to the extent we had hoped for. But one or the other will come as surly as we believe it, for our mind requires we perform the actions necessary to accomplish success or failure.

This is not the "law of attraction" or "The Secret," if you are familiar with them. This is not that you attract that about which you spend your time thinking. Rather, this is simply that your actions are ultimately dictated by your personal beliefs about who you are and what you are capable of doing because your mind won't allow you to rest until you've taken the steps it dictates you take in order to succeed. Your body may want to rest, you mind forces it forward. You don't want to pick up the phone; your mind insists you take action. You thoughts "attract" nothing, but your mind forces you to action until you have achieved.

Consequently, just as basic as desire—maybe more basic—are your personal beliefs about yourself. Those beliefs will determine your ultimate success, although that success may not be defined in the exact terms you want. Moreover, this isn't to deny that outside forces may limit your success, but more limiting than outside forces for most are the internal limitations they place on themselves.

The beliefs that salespeople develop that limit their success have acquired the name "limiting beliefs." As the name implies, they limit the ability of the holder to accomplish certain things they may wish to accomplish.

Limiting beliefs are funny little fellows. They tend to creep into our thinking without being noticed and grow with each small failure or setback. Rarely do they manifest themselves as out and out denials of ability. Such comments as "I can't," "it's not possible," or "it can't be done," are the exception, rather than the rule of what we tell ourselves.

Instead, we modify our limiting beliefs by blaming something we cannot control for preventing our success. We ease into limiting ourselves with subtle excuses such as "I can't do that because (of some outside force)," or "if only I had (some missing talent or trait)."

The reality is that often these are simply excuses we feed ourselves to prevent ourselves from having to accept responsibility for failure, for fear, for our view of who we believe we are and what we believe we are capable of doing.

What we call failure is not the falling down but the staying down.
— **Mary Pickford**

Philosophers, and now psychologists, have debated the question of beliefs and their effect upon our behavior for centuries. Although there are several theories regarding the validity of even the concept of belief, common sense indicates that we not only hold certain beliefs, but those beliefs move us to action—or inaction.

The concept of subject-expectancy effect is closely aligned to our discussion. Subject-expectancy effect is an observation by scientists that some medication recipients who receive a placebo instead of the actual medication report experiencing the beneficial effects of the medication; in addition, there have been documented cases of the placebo having the same verifiable physical effect as the actual drug. *The belief of the recipient of the placebo in the efficaciousness of the anticipated drug produces the results the recipient expected, even to the point that technicians could verify the physical effects the real drug would have produced.*

In social science, it has been observed that subjects who believed they could not accomplish certain tasks would unconsciously sabotage themselves while performing the task, assuring that their expected outcome—failure—was realized. The subject's belief system influenced their performance to such an extent that the subject guaranteed they could not do what they had convinced themselves they could not do, through unconscious self-defeating actions.

Developing a positive self-image and strong positive beliefs about what we can accomplish are vital to becoming a successful salesperson. Our beliefs about who we are and what we can or cannot do derail success or propel us to success.

Everyone has limiting beliefs, those negative beliefs that stymie our actions and their outcomes. These limiting beliefs may have been developed because of our physical appearance, because of past failures, or because of past negative comments or experiences. These beliefs are rooted not in reality, but in our *perception* of ourselves.

Paula: I met Paula several years ago. She sold advertising for an upscale magazine. Her sales career was quite mediocre. She was a slightly below average performer in her company.

Paula had excellent sales skills, was very knowledgeable about her magazine, her market, and the prospects she called on. Her primary problem, like most salespeople, was she just didn't see enough people. Her prospecting activity was well below where it should have been. When she did get in front of prospects, her closing ratio was actually slightly better than most of her associates in the company.

After working with Paula for a little while, it became apparent that her issues weren't in the areas of skills, but in the way she viewed herself in her current position. All of her associates except one were women. The top two salespeople had been models prior to joining the company as sales reps. They are quite simply young, beautiful women. Paula, on the other hand, is about 10 years older than they are and is very nice looking but not "beautiful."

She had convinced herself that her prospects, because of the focus of the magazine on fashion, health, and beauty, expected her to be thin, young, and ravishing. If only she were a little younger, a little thinner, and a little better looking, she would be one of the top performers for her company, she believed.

If only things were a little different she could prospect more, see more people, and sell more advertising. Instead, she invented immense amounts of busy work that just had to be done right then. She had to get this list in order, that ad approved, research this group of prospects before she went out to see them, visit this client, get ready for that show. That darn busy work prevented her from prospecting. She just could never free her schedule enough to hit the streets, as she wanted.

Irrational. Her clients were buying advertising, not her. She was more than presentable. Most any woman in their late thirties would love to look like Paula. However, not Paula as she saw herself in her sales position.

After months of working on her self-image and working to eliminate her limiting beliefs about her looks, Paula had become more confident and less self-conscious. Her prospecting picked up considerably. She was more outgoing at work and with her prospects and clients. Her sales picked up. She edged over the middle of the pack in her company's sales performance. She headed toward the top 40% of sales reps. Then, she left the company.

She is still in advertising. She took a position with another magazine, one that didn't focus on fashion or health.

Paula simply could not free herself of the idea that somehow she didn't measure up to her image of a top sales rep in the fashion/health advertising industry. She had certainly progressed. Her numbers and work ethic demonstrated that. However, she never made the full conversion from her limiting beliefs.

Yet, when she left the magazine and accepted a position with a general interest magazine, she did very well. She is consistently in the top 20% of her company's sales—and at times in the top 10%. In her new position, she doesn't see herself as "the old hag" as she once described herself in her former position.

Despite her efforts to change her limiting beliefs—and her actual success in doing so—she never fully believed she fit within her image of what a fashion/health advertising sales rep should be. Her improved sales and prospecting didn't prove to her satisfaction that her self-image was incorrect. Even though the rest of the world viewed her one way, her limiting beliefs prevented her from being successful until she found a position where her beliefs about herself matched her beliefs about the position.

What are your self-limiting beliefs? What is holding you back? The possibilities are endless. Some don't believe they deserve success. Others, that they are not capable of success. Still others, like Paula, that they have some innate deficiency that they cannot change that affects their ability to succeed.

You may not even be aware of the beliefs you hold about yourself that limit your ability to succeed. That isn't unusual, although we typically have some inkling of what they are.

Whether you are aware of them or not, change can happen. You can reprogram your brain not only to accept success, but also to seek it.

Reprogramming

How do you reprogram yourself to eliminate limiting beliefs and replace them with a belief system that will allow you to pursue and acquire the success you desire? There are a number of reprogramming activities you can employ:

Self-talk: You're in constant conversation with yourself. You think in conversation. You think in words. In addition, as you think, you make judgments, you make plans, and you make decisions. You argue with yourself, you chastise yourself, you praise yourself, and you encourage yourself.

Your internal dialogue has a tremendous affect on what you do and what you believe about the world and yourself. More impact than anyone else can possibly have. No one speaks to you more than you speak to yourself. You are your primary conversation partner. Moreover, you can't turn the conversation off—it goes on constantly. No matter how quiet people may think you are, you are an unceasing chatterbox on the inside.

When discussing outside events and other people with yourself, your conversation may be positive, negative, or neutral. However, when you begin to converse with yourself about yourself, inevitably the conversation is either positive or negative; seldom, if ever, are you neutral. That positive or negative self-talk is determining who you are and what you can or cannot do. It tells you your limitations and your possibilities. It tells you whether you are a jerk or not; whether you are good at what you do or not; whether you have a chance with this next prospect or not; whether you are going to make your numbers this month or not; whether it is even worth spending the time and energy prospecting or not; whether you are going to pick up the phone to make that next cold call or not.

The more negative self-talk you have, the more negative and limiting your beliefs about yourself become. Likewise, the more positive your self-talk, the more positive your image and beliefs about who you are and what you can do.

Since your self-talk is such a powerful influence on your internal belief system, you need to learn to control it, to direct it to be a positive, not negative influence.

Becoming aware of your self-talk is the first step. Monitoring your internal conversation and not allowing the negative thoughts to enter your mind. This is difficult. You may be well into a conversation with yourself before you even realize it. Nevertheless, as soon as you recognize that you're engaging in negative self-talk, you have to force yourself to redirect your thoughts.

If you have just left a prospect where you blew it and you find yourself chastising yourself, change your thoughts. Instead of beating yourself for blowing the interview with the prospect, analyze the mistake to discover how you can correct it. Everyone makes mistakes. Even the superstars have bad meetings with prospects. The problem isn't the bad meeting; it's correcting the mistake and not repeating it.

Again, if you discover you're in the middle of a conversation with yourself about how worthless it is to start calling prospects this morning, cut it off and force yourself to think about how you will succeed in making your calls. Turn your conversation from the negative thoughts about all the rejection you will be receiving to thoughts about how you only need get one or two appointments out of the day's calls. Focus on the small task of getting one appointment, not the task of having to make 100 calls to get that one appointment. Focus on how you can connect with prospects when you get them on the phone, not all of the "wasted" time dialing the phone without talking to anyone.

Be proactive in initiating conversations with yourself about the small victories you had that day, about the things you have done well. Concentrate on the positive things you want to accomplish. Flood your mind with positives. You don't have to make things up. You have many small victories during the day. Concentrate on your victories, not the few losses you may have suffered.

When alone, turn your self-talk from your internal silent talk into spoken language. Speak to yourself aloud. Use all of your senses to help implant your positive self-talk on your brain. Let your brain not only think the thoughts, but let it hear the thoughts. Let your brain hear how successful you are, how well you have done, and how strong a salesperson you are.

As you get better at recognizing your negative self-talk and redirecting it to positive, and as you get used to purposely initiating positive self-talk, you will find your negative self-talk diminishes substantially and your positive self-talk becomes the norm. Instead of discovering yourself in a negative conversation with yourself, you'll discover yourself in positive conversations. At that point, you'll know the process of change has really begun.

Motivation: In an earlier Key, we discussed the problem with outside motivation. It doesn't last. Motivational CD's and speeches tend to motivate for only a short period. However, when learning to reprogram your thinking, listening to motivational CD's often will help to get your thoughts on a more positive track. Since the motivation is short-lived, you must listen often in order to keep the thought pattern going. Nevertheless, while you're in the process of reprogramming your thoughts, listening to motivational CD's every time you get in the car, when you get up in the morning, and before going to bed at night will help you jumpstart your positive self-talk.

You don't need to spend a great deal of cash buying a case full of motivational CD's. Even if you listen to the same CD over and over it will have the effect of starting the positive self-talk. Your purpose is not the motivation the CD purports to offer, but rather the positive internal dialogue with yourself the CD generates.

Self-motivation through repeating affirmations of success also works. By repeating affirmations of success such as "I am a top producing, successful salesperson," "I am a strong, confident, proactive prospector," or "I am the best business consultant in the state," can implant on your brain the positive image you wish to develop. The more specific your affirmation, the more effective it will be. Continually repeating them as both a form of self-motivation and as a statement of fact can reinforce your new image and help erase an old image.

Superstars use affirmations. One of the biggest names in sales training, a gentleman who has been training for decades, who is a household name, who is looked up to and admired by millions, uses affirmations before every presentation he gives. He controls his nervousness and fear by repeating to himself prior to going on stage, "I'm the expert here. I have a message these folks need to hear."

Visualization: Visualizing successfully performing without the fear and negatives you believe about yourself can make success and overcoming negative beliefs more real. Seeing yourself performing as you wish to perform, making the presentations, closing the sales, depositing the commission check can have enormous positive benefit.

Visualization by itself is known as daydreaming. However, visualization in conjunction with other steps to overcome limiting beliefs can be reaffirming and can help to make your changes more concrete.

Some will encourage you to visualize your wildest dreams— buying that Ferrari, moving into that mansion, purchasing the yacht. You may well have moved from visualization back to daydreaming in these instances because they may not be believable to you. However, purchasing a new Lexus, moving into a new home, taking a well-deserved vacation, or putting a swimming pool in the backyard may be a dream that you can believe. Visualize what you can accept as reality. If it's a new Ferrari, great, but if you have to stick with a new Porsche to be believable, then buy the Porsche. If envisioning a six-month cruise around the world is not believable, then envision the two-week cruise through Alaska's bays. What you envision is not important, the success you must attain to acquire your vision is.

Visualize yourself successfully doing the activities a successful salesperson does. See yourself in their role, doing what they do, going where they go, enjoying the things they enjoy.

Write your new belief down: Just as putting goals on paper makes them more real and concrete, writing you new beliefs about yourself on paper makes them more real and concrete.

Reprogramming is more than simply repeating affirmations or monitoring your self-talk. Your new vision and beliefs about yourself must become real; they can't simply be words that you repeat to yourself. Your brain has to convert those words into real beliefs. Hearing the words will help implant them on your mind. Hearing them often will implant them deeper. Nevertheless, seeing them in print is also necessary. Often, your mind will retain what is seen more quickly and will have deeper impact than what is thought or heard. As mentioned above, use all your senses to change your beliefs, immerse yourself in your change.

Once your thoughts reflect what you genuinely want to be, the appropriate emotions and the consequent behavior will flow automatically. Believe it and you will see it.
— **Wayne Dyer**

Act the part to become the part

Act the part to become the part. Changing your self-talk, repeating affirmations, visualizing your success, and writing your new beliefs will change your belief system and, eventually, your actions.

However, waiting for your actions to change is not your best choice. In order to expedite your change in behavior, change your behavior. While working to eliminate your limiting beliefs and replace them with beliefs about yourself that will allow you to achieve the success you want, do what successful salespeople do. Don't wait. Act the part of a successful salesperson to become the successful salesperson you want to be.

Changing is a proactive process. The quickest way to institute change is to work on changing your beliefs and changing your behavior at the same time. They go hand in hand. Changing behavior without working on the underlying beliefs that prevent your success will not be effective. Working on changing your beliefs only will eventually change your behavior, but that delay may be a substantial one. Working on both simultaneously will bring about the desired change much more quickly.

More information:

In a book of this type, there simply isn't enough space to address each topic as fully as one would like. Each of the Keys warrants a full-length book of its own. That being said let me give a couple of resources to help you get deeper into addressing and changing your personal belief system.

Certainly, the best book on the subject is probably Napoleon Hill's *Think and Grow Rich* (Aventine Press, 2004). Despite its age—it was originally published in 1937, the information is still relevant. It may take a little getting used to Hill's writing style, but that is the only deficiency a reader today should find.

A very short but excellent discussion of how your thoughts form your life and how you can take charge of them is Bruce Doyle's *Before You Think Another Thought: An Illustrated Guide to Understanding*

How Your Thoughts and Beliefs Create Your Life (Hampton Roads Publishing Company, 1997). Doyle's book goes further into the realm of new age metaphysics than I am comfortable with, but much of this book is good—including its size, only 128 pages.

Anthony Robbins, *Awaken the Giant Within* (Pocket Books, 2001), covers far more than just dealing with limiting beliefs, but the chapter on beliefs is good. Robbin's approach is from the perspective of Neuro-Linguistic Programming, another new age approach which leaves me a bit out in the cold. In addition, there is an overwhelming amount of self-promotion in the book, almost to the point of being nothing but an infomercial. If you can ignore the self-advertising and you are an adherent of NLP, the chapter on beliefs will help you.

Evaluate Your Beliefs and Establish a Program of Change

If you are not achieving the level of success you want for yourself, examine your beliefs about yourself and your capabilities. Are you sabotaging yourself? Are you unconsciously finding ways to insure you are not successful? What limiting beliefs do you have? Formulate and implement a plan to change your beliefs while, at the same time, taking steps to "act the part to become the part." Change your behavior and your thinking immediately.

Summary

You are on your way to becoming the superstar you want to be. After working your way through all 12 Keys, you now have:

Identified those beliefs that limit your ability to succeed

- You have developed and implemented a program to change those beliefs from negative to positive

- You have begun doing the things successful salespeople do, knowing that your actions and you changing beliefs will bring the success you want

- You have researched your sales history and not only know your sales and marketing numbers, but you know what you must do in order to make the income you seek

- You have researched your strengths and weaknesses using your past sales history, taking formal behavioral assessments, and seeking input from others'

- You have used the information you've discovered about your strengths to develop a marketing plan that focuses on the marketing channels and the marketing methods that take advantage of your strengths and minimizes or even eliminates your weaknesses

- You have adopted a sales process that allows you to use your strengths to their fullest

- You have established a personal training schedule to addresses the sales areas where you need or want improvement

- You have created a prospect and client communication program that will contact your clients and prospects at least 14 times during the year, each contact loaded with added value to train your prospects and clients to pay attention to you, not to ignore you

- You have established a work and career investment schedule that will maximize your time and money investment in your career and still give you the time and freedom to enjoy your family, friends and other pursuits.'

- You have made realistic sales and income projections for the coming year and you know exactly what you must do to reach those objectives'

- You have engaged a mentor and/or hired a personal sales coach to help you reach your full potential

You have done an incredible amount of work. Probably for the first time in your sales career you know exactly where are and how you got here; you know where you have been; and, most importantly, you know where you are going and exactly how you are going to get there.

If you have diligently worked your way through each Key and have implemented each as it is supposed to be implemented, you are truly to be congratulated, as few will do it. Most who read this book will begin, shrug, and go on to something else, always looking for an easier way. You, however, put in the time, you put in the thought and the energy, and you put in place the foundations of a superstar career. I have no doubt you will become the success you desire to be. Your simple dedication in completing each of these exercises indicates the amount of dedication, commitment, and desire you have. You are among the few 10 or 15% who will read this book and actually implement what they have learned.

On the other hand, if you are among the 85 or 90% who decide the effort is simply too great, or the time commitment too large, or the process too difficult, well, at least you know what it takes. It's there for the taking. I hope you find another way. Maybe luck will be on your side, because if you make it to the top, it won't be because you planned it, it will be because you were one of the lucky ones who stumbled into it.

Additional Resources

At www.thetwelvekeys.com/html/limiting_beliefs.html you'll find additional resources and articles relating to changing you beliefs and especially dealing with limiting beliefs.

If you are overwhelmed with the work to be done to create the superstar sales career you seek, you might find that joining a 12 Key Work Group will give you the structure and focus you need. If you would like to consider joining a group, you can find more information at www.thetwelvekeys.com/html/workgroups.html.

Key 13: For Sales Managers, Companies, and Meeting Planners

Nothing focuses the mind better than the constant sight of a competitor who wants to wipe you off the map.
— Wayne Calloway

Without a doubt, all of us, just like Pepsi when Calloway was CEO, have competitors who want to wipe us off the map. No one is insulated from competition. None, no matter how large, can sit back and glory in success.

Yet, competition is only a part of the sales dilemma.

Your sales team is constantly under attack. Not just from your competition, but from themselves, from unrelated products and services that vie for the same dollars, and from buyer apathy, the dreaded choice to do nothing. The world of sales is teaming with roadblocks to your sales team's success and, thus, you company's future.

In addition, many salespeople—and companies--fail to recognize the difference between sales training and product training. To many, they are the same, not realizing the difference and, therefore, neglecting one or the other. Usually sales training is the set of skills left in the cold.

Many companies work diligently to train the members of their sales team. Managers are expected to be trainers; some companies have professional training departments; others encourage their team members to read books and listen to CD's. Still, most companies do not have the time, money, or expertise to provide much, if any, training.

One of the complaints I hear most often from salespeople and managers is the company they work for provides no *useful* training. The focus of company training is on product or service. This makes perfect sense since sales training is transferable from company to company, whereas product or service training goes to the heart of the company. Those products and services are what the company lives to deliver. Moreover, who knows those products and services better than the company who manufactures or provides them?

Yet, I consistently hear a yearning from salespeople that they wish their company would bring in top trainers to address the issues of selling as selling, not selling as product knowledge. These complaints are not exclusive to salespeople from small and mid-size companies who don't have the resources for a professional training department. I hear the same complaints from reps from the some of the world's largest banking, securities, insurance, real estate, mortgage, and high tech firms. I hear the same complaints from top producers and new hires alike.

When I present a public referral selling, prospecting, personal marketing, or 12 Key workshop or seminar for salespeople, I get numerous questions about why their company will not give them this information. Why, they ask, isn't their company giving them real, practical, useful training like this instead of the same old worn material they present? The only answer I can give is that they're either not aware of the material their salespeople want or they're not aware of the training available.

Why else wouldn't a company provide the very training that could change their sales force? Money? I doubt it. Companies spend billions on training. Much of it useless, but it's still expensive.

Is it they just want to withhold the information from their salespeople? Of course, not, they want to sell and will help their salespeople in any manner they can.

From my discussions with managers, executives, and training departments, the most prevalent reason companies don't provide the training their teams really need and want is that they simply don't know what their teams want or, in many cases, need. It's as simple as that. They assume they know and they make their plans and arrangements based on their assumptions.

We May Be Able to Help

McCord and Associates, works with companies, professionals and individual salespeople alike. Our company clients include Fortune 50 companies all the way down to companies with 5 or 6 salespeople.

In addition, we coach individual salespeople and hold seminars and tele-seminars that are open to the public.

Our areas of specialization are prospecting, referral selling, personal marketing, and, of course, the foundational Keys to creating a successful sales career.

Unlike some in the sales training industry, we firmly believe in specialization. Few companies or individuals are competent to provide training in all aspects of sales and marketing. Sales and selling is simply too complicated for any one company, no matter the size or talent, to be able to do a quality job in all areas. Certainly, there are many who claim to do it all. However, few, if any, do a quality job in all areas.

Our focus is simple--helping your sales team increase their production by increasing their pipeline. We address the most critical area salespeople face--the area where more salespeople and companies fail than all other areas combined. Our techniques and strategies are designed to deal with the real world your people face everyday. We are results oriented, not theory oriented. Sales theory is great fun to discuss and argue, but it has never found a prospect or made a sale.

Specifically, our ideal clients are companies with sales teams that are:

- Selling in a relationship based environment
- Each salesperson must prospect for the majority of their clients
- The salesperson does not use a scripted, canned presentation
- Commissions or bonuses are a substantial portion of the salesperson's compensation

Whether you need a quick session during a weekly sales meeting or a three-day workshop/seminar, or anything in-between, we would like the opportunity to discuss with you how we might be able to help your team become more successful. Contact me directly at pmccord@mccordandassociates.com or for general information email info@mccordandassociates.com.

Meeting Planners

Are you responsible for your company, organization, or association's local, state, regional, national or international meeting, conference, convention or retreat? Possibly, you need a strong presence for your booth at a major show? A keynote speaker for your company awards dinner?

Paul McCord is a top speaker who will bring a strong message and the motivation to help your team implement it. Paul is sought after for his workshops, seminars and keynote presentations because his speaking philosophy is to deliver valuable, immediately useable content, not to simply entertain.

Paul speaks on sales prospecting, personal marketing, creating a public image as an expert, overcoming limiting beliefs, and leadership. National clients and local/regional offices such as the National Association of Insurance and Financial Advisors, National City Mortgage, Women's Council of Realtors, Keller Williams Realty, Microsoft, and many others have enjoyed Paul's presentations.

If you are looking for a speaker in North America or worldwide, Paul would like to discuss with you how he can help you make your meeting, convention, or conference one that your attendees will remember. Contact him directly a pmmcord@mccordandassociates.com, or for booking information, contact debbie@mccordandassociates.com. He may also be booked through the National Speakers Exchange www.nationalspeakersxchange.com or Spotlight Speakers Bureau www.spotlightwww.com.

About the Author

$\mathcal{P}$aul McCord is an internationally recognized authority on prospecting, referral selling, and personal marketing. Paul's first book, *Creating a Million Dollar a Year Sales Income: Sales Success through Client Referrals* (John Wiley and Sons, 2007), is quickly becoming recognized as the authoritative work on referral selling.

After graduating from Texas A&M University, Commerce, Paul entered the Doctor of Philosophy program in philosophy at the University of Dallas. Deciding that the real world was more interesting than the Ivory Tower of academia, Paul left the program to tackle the very real world of business.

Over the past two and half decades Paul has sold and managed sales teams selling intangibles such as securities, insurance, mortgages, and advertising both directly to consumers and wholesaling to brokerage and reseller businesses of all sizes.

Paul opened his sales training and consulting firm, McCord and Associates, to address the issues salespeople, professionals and companies face generating new business with his innovative, proven, and effective strategies.

Sharpened by his studies of logic and critical thinking, Paul brings to sales an eye critical of the status quo. During his twenty-five plus years in sales, he has developed new and effective approaches to some of the most critical problems salespeople and companies face in the areas of lead generation, prospecting, personal marketing, and the foundations of a successful career.

His articles appear in business and industry publications throughout the world such as Selling Power newsletters, Advisor Today, The Dallas Morning News, Senior Market Advisor, The Seattle Times, Hotel and Motel Management, Airport Business, Employee Benefit Adviser, Enterprise Week, and many others. In addition, he is quoted and interviewed extensively regarding the issues and opportunities salespeople face in prospecting, referral selling, and marketing.

His blog http://businessresearchdatabase.com/Salesand ManagementBlog/ has been cited as a model for businesses wishing to establish an effective blog. He may be reached at pmccord@ mccordandassociates.com.

Purchasing Multiple Copies of SuperStar Selling

If you need to purchase 10 or more copies for your sales team, company, association, or group, bulk purchase discounts are available by contacting McCord and Associates at 281-216-6845 or info@mccordandassociates.com.

Can You Really Build Your Business from Referrals Like the Mega-producers? YES!

Have you wondered how the mega-producers can generate so many high quality referrals that they can make over a million dollars a year from referral business?

Learn how the mega-producers do it in this systematic guide to generating a huge volume of high quality referrals from your clients and prospects.

Paul McCord has done the research. Now he shows you exactly how you can build your business on referrals, using the same techniques and strategies the mega-producers use.

"The joy that earns this book a rare 5 stars is the practical, thorough and innovative treatment of referrals."

— David Straker, Business Methodology Consultant, National Assessment Agency, UK

"What a breath of fresh air. Finally, a sales book that is not only practical, but actually produces results."

— Lonnie Timmons, Sales Manager, Gresham Toyota, Gresham, CA.

"This book lays out in systematic detail the most effective selling and referral system I've seen. It doesn't make getting referrals easy but it makes getting them predictable."

**— Dave Lakhani, Best-selling author,
Persuasion: The Art of Getting What You Want**

"This is one of those books every salesperson should read and keep by their desk and constantly refer to."

**— Stu Taylor, Nationally Syndicated Radio Host,
Equity Strategies**

**Available at Barnes and Noble, Borders, Amazon,
and all fine booksellers.**

Need Added Structure Working through $uper$tar $elling?

The $uper$tar $elling Workbook
Will Help You Focus Your Work

Working through each Key can become difficult and even overwhelming. Although the book takes you step-by-step through the process, you may find you need more structure than the book can provide.

If so, you have options.

Joining a 12 Key Work Group will allow you to work your way through the program with Paul McCord helping and directing you each step of the way.

However, if you prefer working at your own pace, the companion Workbook will give you added structure and guidance as you work through each Key.

Designed to be used by individual salespeople or in small, self-guided groups, the workbook has forms, examples, and additional resources to help you implement each of the Keys. Easy to use 8 ½ X 11 format.

Available at www.thetwelvekeys.com/html/workbook.html, the workbook can be purchased individually for $29.95. For purchases by companies or groups of 10 or more, discount pricing is available. For group purchase, contact McCord and Associates at workbook@mccordandassociates.com

Printed in the United States
103065LV00002B/101/A